The Eagles of Crete

An Untold Story of Civil War

Colin Janes

Copyright © 2013 Colin Janes
All rights reserved.

ISBN: 1-4819-5898-4
ISBN-13: 9781481958981

Contents

1	Occupation	1
2	Collaborators are Eliminated	17
3	Civil War Looms	31
4	Fighting in the East	45
5	Unrest in the West	61
6	The Evacuation of the Villages	77
7	Government Minister Ambushed	93
8	The Battle in the Samaria Gorge	109
9	The Guerrilla Force Disintegrates	125
10	The Net Tightens	143
11	The Perfect Hiding Place	157
12	Decision to Disband	173
13	The Eagles of Crete	193
Bibliography		207
List of Main Characters		209
Glossary		213

Chapter 1
Occupation

On 6 April 1941, a month after British and Anzac troops had landed in Piraeus, four German columns swarmed across the Bulgarian frontier into Greece. Greek troops resisted gallantly but, within days of the invasion, Salonika and the ports of Thrace were captured. Other German divisions entered Greece via Yugoslavia and serious resistance collapsed when the Greek army on the Albanian front was encircled and its generals surrendered on 21 April.

British and Commonwealth soldiers fought a series of stubborn rearguard actions as they made their retreat, without air cover, towards Attica. Hurried plans were made for the evacuation of the Allied troops. Following two days of German air attacks, Piraeus had suffered extensive damage and was unusable so the men were directed to a number of small ports and evacuation beaches, mainly in the Peloponnese.

On 18 April, Prime Minister Koryzis shot himself and King George II replaced him with Emmanuel Tsouderos, a Cretan. The king made a radio broadcast from Athens on 22 April stating that the Greeks would fight to the end and the following day departed with members of his government for the mountainous stronghold of Crete.

Evacuation of the troops from the Greek mainland took place on the four nights of 24–28 April. More than 22,000 men were evacuated to Egypt and another 19,000 were taken to Crete. The Greek navy, consisting of a cruiser, six destroyers and four submarines, escaped to Alexandria.

In the chaos caused by the rapid German advance, around seven hundred communists fled their prisons and islands of exile. The most successful escape was in early May from Folegandros, whence about a hundred political exiles made their getaway, with the majority heading for Athens. A group of eight Cretans and one mainlander seized a boat and set sail in the opposite direction, for Crete. They intended, on arrival, to put themselves at the disposal of the authorities on the island and to offer their help in resisting the invader.

The leader of this group was 33-year-old Nikos Manousakis from Viannos. Manousakis had been sentenced to an indefinite prison term on Folegandros for persistent attempts to organise strikes and for printing and distributing literature on behalf of the Greek Communist Party (KKE). The son of the local mayor, Manousakis had gone to Athens University in 1928 to study law, but on joining the KKE he gave up his studies and worked as a clerk in an Athens factory. In 1936 he was arrested and exiled to Folegandros.

When their boat arrived in Heraklion harbour it immediately attracted the attention of the police. As soon as the nine men disembarked they were surrounded on the quayside and on identifying themselves were promptly arrested. Despite their protests, they were temporarily locked up in the local jail and did not gain their release until the Germans started to bomb Heraklion, a few days later.

On 20 May 1941, the Germans began their invasion of Crete, landing parachutists at Maleme, Rethymnon and Heraklion. The parachutists suffered heavy casualties but after two days of fighting had control of Maleme airfield. Reinforcements were flown in to Maleme and the Germans gradually increased their foothold on the island. Cretan civilians flocked to join the Allies in defending their homes and fought side by side with Allied troops.

By 27 May, the Allied position in western Crete was judged to be hopeless and all troops in the Canea area were ordered to retreat over the White Mountains to the village of Hora Sfakion on the south coast. Villagers on their route continued to assist the Allies while at the same time appealing to them for weapons with which to carry on the struggle against the Germans. Young men and boys collected all the cases of ammunition and rifles that were discarded by the retreating troops and hid them for use at a later date.

On the night of 28/29 May the Allied garrison in Heraklion, numbering around 4,000 men, was evacuated by sea without intervention

The Eagles of Crete

from the German paratroopers in the area. Allied troops received their instructions several hours before their intended departure and destroyed all the military equipment they could not take with them. At the last moment they carried out an orderly withdrawal to the harbour where two Royal Navy cruisers and six destroyers arrived a few hours after dark.

As the fighting in Crete drew to a close the Italians landed unopposed at Sitia, in the peaceful eastern prefecture of Lasithi. Crete had fallen but during the fighting many weapons had been captured from the enemy and at the end of the battle the Cretans were better armed than they had been when the fighting started.

On the night that the Allied troops were making their departure for Egypt, the Folegandros escapees met together in a house in a suburb of Heraklion and agreed on the formation of a resistance organisation, membership of which was to be open to all patriotic Greeks who wished to join the fight against the occupying forces, regardless of ideological convictions. To muster support, they set out for their native villages throughout the island.

Despite the large number of arrests made during General Metaxas' dictatorship many KKE members had remained at liberty. Throughout Greek towns and villages there were networks of communists in contact with each other, and their experience of working clandestinely ensured that they would quickly adapt to the conditions of the occupation. It was these people that the escapees set out to contact.

Gavdos, one of the most arid and remote Greek islands, lying 26 nautical miles south of Hora Sfakion, was regarded by General Metaxas as an ideal place of exile for some of the most senior opponents of his regime. Life was hard for the exiles on the almost barren, malarial island that had a boat connection with Hora Sfakion every three weeks at most. There were no books, writing materials or medical care, and little news from the outside world.

As the Germans advanced into Crete, the number of Allied soldiers retreating from the Canea sector to the south coast increased daily. Royal Navy ships arrived at Hora Sfakion to evacuate the men to Egypt but only came at night to avoid enemy aircraft. Troops desperate to avoid capture put to sea in any type of vessel thought likely to make it to safety.

One morning at the end of May, a small rowing boat arrived at Sarakiniko Bay on Gavdos. Its crew of Greek soldiers disembarked and hurried off for the south of the island where, according to rumour, a British warship was moored, awaiting nightfall to evacuate troops to Egypt.

As soon as dusk fell, seven communist exiles seized the rowing boat. Mitsos Vlandas, a Cretan from Marathos near Heraklion, who had been on Gavdos for a year, took charge of the escape.

It was impossible to cover the distance to Crete in the small boat in a single night so the seven men put in at the small island of Gavdopoula, a few kilometres away, before dawn broke. Dragging the boat ashore they hid it as best they could. All day they waited on Gavdopoula watching the German planes patrolling the sea off Crete searching for ships and boats taking Allied troops to Egypt. At twilight the men pushed the boat into the water once more.

There was a strong current and all night they struggled with the oars, making very slow progress. Eventually, late the next morning, they reached dry land, a few kilometres to the east of Hora Sfakion. They were exhausted and desperately thirsty. To ascertain the latest military situation they set off for the nearest village, where they were told that the officer in command of the Allied troops had surrendered to the Germans the previous day.

The escapees concocted the story that they were officers and soldiers from a Greek regiment that had been fighting the Germans but had now disbanded. There were scores of men in a similar situation and they were readily believed by the villagers.

To be less conspicuous, the escapees agreed to split up and rendezvous at Marathos in two weeks' time. Travelling through the island by separate routes also gave them a better opportunity for gathering more information and renewing any former contacts they had.

Vlandas proceeded directly to Marathos, which he reached in three days. His mother had died two years earlier while he was in the Acronauplia prison but he was soon reunited with his father and brother, neither of whom he had seen for several years. A few days later he was in contact with the KKE leadership in Heraklion.

News of Vlandas' arrival soon reached Nikos Manousakis, the escapee from Folegandros, at his home in Viannos. Manousakis set off immediately to join up with his comrades from Gavdos.

In the middle of June, two weeks after the surrender of Crete, a small gathering was held in a cave in a gorge near Agios Sillas. Present were the seven escapees from Gavdos, five of those who had escaped from Folegandros and a handful of local communists. At the meeting, the formation of a resistance movement was approved and Nikos Manousakis was elected its leader.

A month later another meeting was held and communists from every part of Crete were in attendance. Word was slowly spreading that several veteran communists had landed on Crete and had established a resistance movement. The main decision taken at this meeting was to send a representative to western Crete to find General Mandakas, who was hiding in the White Mountains, and offer him the position of Commander-in-Chief.

With the nucleus of a resistance movement established, Vlandas was anxious to reach Athens. The Germans were meticulously checking passengers on all vessels to the mainland but Vlandas arranged with a local captain to replace one of the crew on a caique bound for Piraeus. He successfully managed to pass himself off as a sailor and in late summer Vlandas arrived in Piraeus. It was to be three years before he returned to Crete.

Meanwhile, Nikos Manousakis set about the job of finding General Mandakas, who had been on the run for the past three years. Born in Lakki, a large village in the hills south of Canea, Manoli Mandakas was the son of a famous guerrilla leader who had fought for the island's independence from the Turks. To mark the union of Crete with Greece, his father, Anagnostis Mandakas, had been given the honour of raising the Greek flag at the Firka fortress in Canea in the presence of King Constantine I and Prime Minister Eleftherios Venizelos, the founder of the country's Liberal Party. One of twelve children, Manoli had joined the army in 1910 and taken part in the Balkan Wars in 1912–13, seen service in World War I and had later served in the Asia Minor campaign.

In 1935, Mandakas had been promoted to general but was cashiered from the army that year following a failed coup attempt. He returned to his native Crete but in 1938 became implicated in another coup, this time against the Metaxas Government. At Easter a group of army officers in Athens had plotted an uprising that was to take place at the end of July. The plan was for rebellion to break out throughout the country but when the day for the coup arrived it was only in the Canea prefecture in Crete that any action was taken.

At midnight on the appointed day the signal was given and the church bells rung in the villages around Canea. Villagers armed themselves with guns, swords, clubs and knives and made for the town. The gendarmes in Canea offered no resistance and were disarmed. All public buildings were occupied and the governor's house surrounded but the rebels failed to cut off the telephones and the governor rang Athens for reinforcements later that morning. When it became clear to the rebels in Canea that no action had been taken in the rest of Greece they quickly returned to their villages.

The small band of leaders responsible for the Canea rebellion went into hiding. A few weeks later several of them accepted an offer made by Metaxas and took a boat to Cyprus, where they went into self-imposed exile. Mandakas took to the mountains; his wife, Maria, was banished to Milos with their two children.

While in hiding, General Mandakas was helped by the island's many Liberals but he also had the advantage of receiving support from all local KKE members as his wife was the sister of one of the most senior KKE leaders on Crete. Although not a communist, Mandakas was respected by left-wingers for his uncompromising stand against General Metaxas.

In the late summer of 1941, Manousakis finally met the general near Lakki and offered him command of the military wing of the resistance movement. The 50-year-old general accepted without hesitation.

The occupation forces lost no time in tightening their grip on the island. Leaflets were dropped by plane announcing that the Allied soldiers who were still at large should be handed over and not given refuge by the population. The penalty for those caught aiding Allied troops would be death. Weapons of all types, including hunting rifles, were to be handed in to the nearest military post immediately. Those not complying with this order were liable to be shot.

Mules were requisitioned from villages and men were rounded up for fatigue duties. In the early days of the occupation the Germans would surround a village during the night and at first light assemble all men and boys between the ages of sixteen to seventy and take them to where labour was needed. Gangs were required to dig trenches, build fortifications, break up rocks into gravel for road building and to load and unload the cargoes in the harbours. Later, the Germans used the help of community leaders to select villagers for the working parties by introducing a rota system. If the workers failed to show up for work the community had to pay a fine, which was usually a set amount of olive oil or a number of sheep. Threats were made that, if the fine were not paid, houses in the villages would be blown up. The Cretans hated the idea of working for the Germans but seeing that they could not avoid it, they contrived to do as little work as possible when they found themselves dragooned into forced labour for the enemy.

In Canea, the capital of Crete at that time, a curfew and blackout were imposed between the hours of sunset to sunrise and were strictly enforced. Assembly was banned and a special permit was required for printing presses. Newspapers were censored and orders given that the Cretans were allowed to tune in only to Greek or German radio stations; severe penalties were announced for those caught listening to the BBC. All motor vehicles had to be registered with the German authorities and large buildings were requisitioned for use by the occupying forces as offices or to house high officials. Schools were taken over for use as barracks and the market was converted into a warehouse, storing food, clothing and footwear. Flour from the mills was confiscated for the use of the army. Bread from the bakeries that were working for the Germans was available on the black market but the price demanded, in cigarettes, soap, olive oil or eggs, was a high one. Food was more plentiful in the countryside and those who could do so fled to the villages where they had relatives.

In the early months of the occupation the Cretans paid a heavy price for resisting the invader. The villages where resistance had been fiercest were burnt and many of the male inhabitants executed. Concern at the reprisals prompted several local dignitaries to get together and approach the mayor, Major Nikos Skoulas, to ask him to use his influence with the Germans to obtain a general amnesty and an end to the reign of terror. A former gendarme officer, Skoulas arranged for a delegation of eminent citizens - mostly doctors and lawyers - to meet General Waldemar Andrae, the newly appointed commander of Crete.

The meeting achieved its goal. On 9 September the German military attaché arrived from Athens with orders for a general amnesty to take immediate effect and a deadline for the surrender of all weapons was set for the end of September. The number of Cretans executed from the beginning of the invasion up until 9 September was put at 1,135. With the announcement of the general amnesty, a relative peace settled over Crete.

At the beginning of the occupation the Cretans could do little more than show their defiance by helping the Allied soldiers who were still at large. Of the hundreds of soldiers hiding on Crete some were stragglers who had become separated from their units during the battle and others had taken to the hills after the departure of the final evacuation ship. Escapees from the temporary prison camps soon added to their number.

News that there were large numbers of troops in hiding in Crete began to trickle through to Cairo as some of the men left on the island managed to make their way to North Africa in small caiques. On the night of 26 July a British officer landed by submarine on the south coast near Preveli Monastery to arrange for the evacuation of the men.

Within a month 200 Allied troops had been rounded up, crammed into two submarines, and transported to Egypt.

Other British officers followed with orders to contact and attempt to unite the various small resistance groups that were springing up throughout the island. But the evacuation of their men was the priority. Guerrilla movements were urged to refrain from any action until the stragglers were safely away.

As winter set in the problems of evacuating the stragglers increased. When Captain Alexander Fielding arrived in Crete by submarine in the early hours of 12 January 1942 strong winds forced him ashore a few kilometres to the west of his intended landing place at Tris Ekklisies. Fielding and the small party with him struggled to get to dry land and were unable to inform the 120 men awaiting evacuation of the change of rendezvous.

For several weeks the men had been hiding out near Tris Ekklisies. Two attempts to drop food and supplies to them by air had failed. The Germans captured the whole of one drop that fell near Agii Deka and only half of another load that was dropped on the northeast of the Mesaras Plain reached the hungry stragglers. The airdrops confirmed German suspicions that a large number of Allied troops were hiding in the area awaiting a boat to Egypt. German search parties descended on the coast and a few of the men were caught; most evaded capture and scattered westwards.

Eight months after the surrender of the island there were still an estimated 300 Allied troops on Crete being looked after by local villagers who gave freely what little they had, with no expectation of repayment. Food was short for everybody and the stragglers, many of whom were now barefoot and dressed in rags, continued to spend a miserable winter in the open. The last group of fifty men was finally evacuated from Crete in May 1943, two years after the fall of the island.

By late 1941 all the small resistance parties that had sprung up in Rethymnon prefecture had come under the authority of Lt. Colonel Christos Tziphakis, a retired gendarme officer who had commanded the local resistance to the paratroopers. Captain Fielding, who had established himself above Asi Gonia, met Tziphakis at the home of a wealthy villager in Prines and was immediately impressed with Tziphakis' knowledge of German movements and dispositions in the area. Tziphakis readily agreed to cooperate with the British.

Fielding now turned his attention to Canea, where several members of a fledgling spy network were being arrested at regular intervals. Before the war he had lived in Cyprus and spoke fluent Greek but he had never visited the town before. Andreas Polentas, a lawyer from Vrisses, agreed to go with Fielding as his guide.

The pair had no difficulty getting into Canea unchallenged. They chose to go by bus: buses were seldom stopped and checked as thoroughly at roadblocks as travellers arriving on foot, and they managed to meet some of the town's leading figures. Among these was Nikos Skoulas, the mayor, who was taken by surprise by Fielding in his office in the Town Hall. Skoulas agreed to help the resistance as best he could.

Throughout the rest of the island, the handful of British officers who were now arriving in Crete had slowly been making contact with military leaders they considered reliable. They planned to set up an organisation to help them in their intelligence work, using men from a military background where possible.

On 2 October 1942, Captain Dunbabin, the senior Allied liaison officer on the island, held a meeting with several Cretan army officers at Agios Mironas, a few kilometres south of Heraklion, and a new resistance group, The National Organisation of Cretans (EOK), was established. Membership of EOK was open to all except known communists. This new organisation was officially recognised by the Greek government-in-exile a few months later. The British undertook to provide members of EOK with weapons, uniforms and boots but made it clear that they did not want a military rising on Crete: the primary purpose of EOK was to provide information, messengers and guards for the British officers and their radio stations.

In Lasithi, the prefecture under the Italians, the leading member of EOK was Colonel Plevres; in Heraklion, Major Beteinakis; and in Rethymnon, Colonel Tziphakis. In Canea, the obvious choice would have been General Mandakas, but Mandakas was unacceptable to King George II and the Greek government-in-exile because of his communist connections. Eventually, Major Emmanuel Nikoloudes was selected to lead EOK in Canea.

On the mainland, The National Liberation Front (EAM) had been formed on 27 September 1941. Ostensibly this was a coalition of several small parties but in reality it was dominated behind the scenes by communists. A military wing of the organisation, The National Popular Liberation Army (ELAS) was set up on 10 April 1942. On learning of the formation of EAM and ELAS the communist leaders in Crete changed the names of their own organisations to EAM/ELAS. There were now two resistance movements in Crete: EOK, which was backed by the British, and EAM/ELAS with ties to the communists on the mainland.

As far as many members of EAM/ELAS were concerned, EOK was a mere tool of the British who armed its members and paid them in gold sovereigns while EAM received nothing. Gradually, EOK increased its numbers but its popular support in Crete during the occupation, especially in the Canea prefecture, never rivalled that of EAM/ELAS.

In Athens, on 23 February 1943, EAM set up the National Panhellenic Youth Organisation (EPON) which was aimed at all Greeks, male and female, between the ages of fifteen and twenty-two. A similar organisation had already been established in Crete and this was now renamed EPON.

Local members of EPON were soon very active in the town of Canea, daubing slogans on the walls and in the roads and spreading the news they had gleaned from secretly listening to the BBC. This was dangerous work but much appreciated by the townspeople who had no news on the progress of the war apart from that provided by the Germans.

Another of the EPONites' duties was to distribute leaflets that were printed on a press that was kept in a ruined, damp Turkish bath in the Kastelli quarter of town. The only entrance to this *hamam* was through a hole in the roof, from which hung a rope ladder. When the press was not in use this entrance was blocked off and secured with a strong chain. The leaflets denounced traitors, collaborators and those involved in the black market and publicised the names of the victims of the Germans.

On 8 September 1943 there was great excitement throughout Crete at the news that the Italians had signed an armistice and the war with Italy was at an end. The Italians had two divisions in Lasithi prefecture and many of the 32,000 Italian troops celebrated what they thought was the end of the war by going to the taverns and getting drunk.

The Germans, however, were well prepared for the Italian armistice. On its announcement, General Friedrich Muller was appointed to take over Lasithi and German troops moved in quickly to seize strategic points in the prefecture, disarming the Italians as they did so. Muller gave the Italians three alternatives: join the Germans and fight alongside them; surrender their weapons and work for the Germans as non-combatants; or be interned.

Two Italian battalions took to the hills above Sitia but shortage of food in the villages soon compelled the men to return to their units. Eighty rifles and a few cases of hand-grenades were handed over to the Cretans but within two weeks of the armistice the Germans were in complete control of Lasithi. A small group of Italian officers who had expressed a desire to resist the Germans was rounded up. After a time, many of the Italians who had surrendered their weapons and taken on non-combatant duties found their rations so poor that they rejoined their units and took up arms once again.

The Italian surrender forced the Germans in Crete to spread their forces more thinly throughout the whole of the island. As the Germans began to regroup, withdrawing small garrisons and outposts in the countryside, they conceded a greater freedom of movement to those working against them.

Crete had been relatively peaceful for two years but the Italian armistice led to a serious outbreak of fighting and reprisals. Manoli Bandouvas, a native of Ano Asites, had been born into humble peasant stock but before the war had become one of the wealthiest and most influential local landowners. Armed by the British, Bandouvas had been in the mountains since the Battle of Crete and had his own private army of followers. Convinced that an Allied invasion and liberation were only days away, he ordered a general mobilisation of the Cretans. To the horror of the British officers, he received support from Colonel Beteinakis, the EOK leader in Heraklion.

Bandouvas' guerrillas killed two German soldiers as they collected potatoes outside Kato Simi. A collaborator ran to inform the Germans of the killings while Bandouvas and his band, which had numbered 80 at the beginning of the year but had recently grown to 300, proceeded to destroy two small guard posts at Viannos and Arvi.

On 15 September, 2,000 German troops arrived at Viannos in 150 trucks, cordoned off the area and set about rounding up the male population. Seven villages were destroyed or partly destroyed and 451 men were shot in front of their families. The bodies of the dead were left for five days before the Germans allowed the relatives to bury them.

Bandouvas and his men scattered westwards but were unable to find villages willing to shelter them. Many of the most recent recruits went home. A small band of communists, who had previously worked with Bandouvas, broke away and reappeared in the mountains shortly afterwards under the leadership of Yanni Podias.

With German patrols on his heels, Bandouvas headed west, marching by night and resting during the daytime, and reached Mount Tsilivdikas six days later. As the eighty-strong guerrilla band relaxed on the slopes of the mountain one morning, lookouts spotted a small German search party approaching their hide-out. Bandouvas' men set an ambush and in the ensuing skirmish all the Germans were captured or killed. From one of the captives, a Cretan in German uniform, they learnt that a large German force was in the area and that they were virtually surrounded.

That evening, under cover of a thick mist, the guerrillas escaped the encirclement. Bandouvas and his men spent the next few days dodging enemy patrols as they made their way through Kallikratis to Kali Lakki in the White Mountains. News of his reckless attack on the Germans had gone before him and Bandouvas received a cool reception. He was persuaded to leave the area and he made his way back towards Mount Tsilivdikas. Bandouvas was evacuated from the nearby beach of Rodakino at the end of October.

After Bandouvas' departure, the Germans had considerable success in rounding up the EOK leaders. In Heraklion, Beteinakis was betrayed and captured. Several of his senior officers were arrested and a week later Colonel Plevres was taken into custody in Lasithi. Of the thirty officers arrested, six, including Beteinakis, were sentenced to death and shot. The rest, Plevres among them, were released. A rumour spread that Plevres had earned his release by convincing the Germans that his movement was anti-communist and that he would serve the Germans by fighting ELAS. From then on, the British officers and his fellow Cretans regarded Plevres with some suspicion.

In Canea, the EOK leader, Major Nikoloudes, was arrested and taken to Agia jail. The mayor, Nikos Skoulas, received a tip-off that he was on a wanted list and went into hiding in the mountains above his native village of Lakki.

A few weeks after the Italian armistice, there was general agreement that the leadership of EOK and EAM-ELAS should get together for a conference to discuss ways of preventing civil conflict breaking out in Crete. On the mainland, civil war - which was to last for five months before a truce was signed - had recently broken out between the two main resistance groups and there was a fear that this could spread to Crete. Messages to Skoulas and Mandakas received favourable replies and a meeting was arranged for the night of 6/7 November 1943.

The gathering of the resistance leaders took place at a farmhouse in the hills between Therisso and Meskla. Skoulas arrived from his mountain hide-out and other senior EOK figures, including Constantine Mitsotakis, a young lawyer, came from Canea. Nikos Manousakis and General Mandakas, represented EAM-ELAS and local EAM leaders from Canea were also present.

After a long night of discussion, a proclamation was issued stating that both sides had agreed to work together to fight the Germans. To achieve this objective most effectively a committee of six men – three from EAM and three from EOK – was to be formed under the presidency of General Mandakas, who commanded great respect throughout the island and was recognised as the man most likely to be able to unite both groups against a common enemy.

Shortly afterwards, however, Mandakas was summoned to the mainland by the EAM leadership and left by fishing boat in mid-December.

Chapter 2
Collaborators are Eliminated

Small groups of ELAS guerrillas first appeared in the White Mountains in western Crete in the summer of 1943. One band, led by Nikos Tsamantis, was made up of men mostly from the village of Meskla. Another band, led by Manoli Pissadakis, was drawn chiefly from the villagers of Samonas and Melidoni.

In the early weeks of resistance, the guerrillas had no permanent base but ranged between Melidoni, Ramni, Drakona, Zourva and Lakki. This was ideal country for the guerrillas as a large part of the area was covered by forest and there were numerous caves to use for hide-outs and many springs that provided water.

Following the Italian armistice, in the autumn of 1943, a number of men took their guns from their hiding places and gathered near remote villages. However, some of the exuberant younger guerrillas held target practice during the daytime and their presence soon became known to the Germans, who mounted an operation against them. For a few days the guerrillas were chased around the mountains but the Germans soon tired of the futility of the hunt. By the time winter came, all the small guerrillas had joined forces and were based near Meskla.

The first noteworthy victory achieved by ELAS in Crete was the destruction of the Jagdkommando led by Sonderfuhrer Fritz Schubert. Schubert was born to Greek-speaking parents but brought up in Germany and had joined the Nazi Party at a young age. Following Bandouvas' attack on the Germans at Kato Simi, Schubert was ordered to form a special unit, made up of Cretans in German uniform, to combat the increasing threat from the guerrillas. At its peak, this unit numbered around 100 men, several of whom were criminals who had agreed to serve the Germans in return for their freedom. Almost half of the men in this unit, known to the Cretans as the Schuberai, came from the village of Kroussonas and were relatives or friends of the local mayor, who had been assassinated as a collaborator by Bandouvas' guerrillas.

The Schuberai made their first appearance in Lasithi immediately after the Italian armistice. They terrorised the villagers and killed more than a dozen men in Kritsa and seven in Tzermiado before moving westwards in pursuit of Bandouvas. Following the skirmish on Mount Tsilivdikas, the Schuberai burnt the villages of Kallikratis and Kali Sikia. Twenty men and nine women were killed at Kallikratis and several more murdered in Kali Sikia. Many of the Schuberai took the opportunity, while in German service, to settle old scores and kill personal enemies, and others looted the property of wealthy farmers.

Having unleashed the Schuberai on the civil population, the Germans soon realised that they had little control over them. General Brauer is reported to have summoned Schubert and reprimanded him after the brutal murders at Kallikratis and Kali Sikia, where women were thrown into the flames of their burning homes. Most of the German officers disliked Schubert and his methods and favoured a more conciliatory approach to the Cretans. By the middle of December, only three months after the unit's formation, the majority of the Schuberai had second thoughts about their actions and many of them deserted, including one of Schubert's bodyguards, who had previously refused an amnesty offered by the guerrillas in return for murdering his leader.

On 1 January 1944, Schubert and fourteen of his men took a truck and drove to Meskla. They parked their vehicle a kilometre from the village and two of the Schuberai, wearing plain clothes, left their weapons in the truck and walked into the village.

The two men went to the *kapheneion*, where they announced that they were from the east of the island and had been members of Bandouvas' band before he left for Egypt. The band, they said, had mostly dispersed after their leader's departure and their village had been burnt as a reprisal for Bandouvas' attack on the Germans. All they wanted now, they declared, was to join the local ELAS unit and continue the struggle against the Germans.

The Eagles of Crete

Meanwhile, Nikos Tsamantis and Manoli Pissadakis, who were just outside Meskla with their men, heard that two strangers had arrived in the *kapheneion* and set off to hear their story first-hand. They soon became suspicious of the men's tale and the two strangers were overpowered and thoroughly searched. German identity cards were found and the two men promptly confessed that they were members of Schubert's unit and that Schubert himself was waiting near the village with a dozen of his men. A messenger was dispatched to fetch all the guerrillas who were outside Meskla and all the ELAS reservists in the village were called to arms.

The Schuberai who were patiently waiting outside Meskla suddenly found themselves under attack from almost 200 armed men. In the ensuing brief gunfight, three of them were killed and another three were captured; Schubert and his six remaining men made their escape to Canea.

The five prisoners were taken up into the mountains above Zourva to the shepherds' encampment at Voulisma. A Guerrilla Court was hastily convened, with Pissadakis as president, and the prisoners were given a trial. The men could not deny their guilt and their appeals for mercy were to no avail. They were condemned as traitors and executed and their bodies were thrown down a pothole.

Ten days after this setback, Schubert and what remained of his unit were transferred to the mainland. The dissolution of Schubert's unit in Crete brought great prestige to ELAS, and many German officers were privately pleased to see the back of the unit and its leader.

But the Germans could not allow the ELAS success to go unchallenged. Early one morning, six weeks after Schubert's defeat at Meskla, a force of 1,500 Germans surrounded the villages of Meskla, Therisso, Zourva, Lakki and Fournes. Over 100 men were arrested and taken to Maleme airfield, where they were put on planes to Athens. Thence they were sent to Germany by train and spent the rest of the war in concentration camps.

One of those arrested in this operation was Manoli Pissadakis, who had spent the night in a house in Zourva. Taken by surprise early in the morning, he managed to hide his weapon before being rounded up. He concealed his true identity by claiming to be in the area looking for some goats to buy, and this saved his life. Only 30 of the hostages arrested that day and taken to Germany survived the war and returned to Crete. One of the survivors was Pissadakis.

On the mainland, in 1943, the Germans had started to form Security Battalions of Greeks who were prepared to fight alongside the Germans against ELAS. The Greeks who joined the Security Battalions did not regard themselves as collaborators but rather as patriots who were fighting Communism; ELAS guerrillas regarded them as traitors.

In Crete the Germans had failed to find a leader for a Security Battalion so had proposed instead the formation of a Special Gendarmerie to deal with sheep thieves and keep law and order in the mountains. Nobody was fooled by the name and recognised that this unit would be nothing more than a Security Battalion to be used against ELAS. In February 1944, Major Dimitri Papayannakis was appointed commander of the Special Gendarmerie in Canea prefecture.

Major Dimitri Papayannakis had been a staunch supporter of Metaxas and was strongly anti-communist. EOK voiced no opposition to Papayannakis and Captain Ciclitira, who had relieved Fielding as senior British officer in the White Mountains, while noting in a report to Cairo that Papayannakis had a history of involvement in the black market, believed he would act independently of the Germans and do little harm. Following his appointment, Ciclitira met Papayannakis, who made it clear that he was prepared to take orders from the British officers if called upon to do so, and, as a token of goodwill, presented Ciclitira with a gendarme uniform to assist him in moving around.

Papayannakis' gendarmes – the men became known as the Papayannaii – numbered around 200 and were lightly armed by the Germans. Many of those who joined the force were, according to ELAS, sheep thieves, looters, ex-jailbirds and villagers made desperate by starvation during the occupation. British officers agreed in their reports to Cairo that the unit contained "many bad hats".

The first confrontation between ELAS and the Papayannaii occurred at the end of March 1944, a month after the unit's formation. A patrol of Papayannaii passed through Kambi one morning and began to ascend the mountains in its search for certain shepherds who were known to be assisting ELAS. A messenger from Kambi ran to *Kapetan* Kriton Kianidis, who was in charge of all ELAS forces in the area, to give him details of the gendarmes' movements.

Born in Athens, Kianidis had served as a cavalry officer fighting the Italians on the Albanian front but in early 1941 he and his men had been transferred to an infantry unit near Kilkis. When the Germans invaded Greece, he retreated with his men southwards and eventually found a caique in the Khalkidhiki that took him to Heraklion. Wounded in the Battle of Crete, he was hospitalised, and married the young woman who nursed him back to health. In the summer of 1943 he took to the mountains and joined ELAS.

Kianidis gave orders for an ambush to be prepared on the path the Papayannaii were known to be taking from Kambi to Samonas. The guerrillas slightly outnumbered the Papayannaii, estimated at forty-strong, and planned to use the element of surprise to achieve a quick, bloodless victory. Kianidis instructed the guerrillas not to shoot to kill unless resistance was offered.

As the Papayannaii came along the path towards Samonas, the youngest guerrilla stepped out from behind an olive tree in front of them. The young man shouted to the sergeant major in charge that he and his men were surrounded and told them to lay down their weapons. A few shots were fired into the air by the guerrillas and the sergeant major and his men did as they were bidden. The guerrillas collected the gendarmes' rifles and ordered them to hand over their boots.

The captured gendarmes were marched up to some shepherds' huts in the mountains where they were berated by Kianidis for bringing dishonour on themselves and their families by collaborating with the Germans. When it grew dark all of the Papayannaii were released except for one man from Kissamos. This man, known to several of the guerrillas as a traitor who had killed EAM supporters, was given a trial by the guerrillas, found guilty and executed.

To avoid the German patrols sent in pursuit of them, the guerrillas moved higher into the mountains, split into smaller groups and scattered. The Germans took their revenge on those who did not flee. Samonas was burnt and 35 prisoners were rounded up and taken to Agia prison.

Major Papayannakis used the German-controlled local paper, the *Paratiritis*, to express his view that all those who took part in the national resistance movement should be executed as anarchists and traitors. The major called on the local population to inform against all known members of the KKE and threatened that if communists continued to escape arrest, their families and relatives, regardless of age or sex, should be seized in their place.

The Papayannaii had often assisted the Germans in rounding up suspects, especially in the town, but their most infamous deed was the murder of Lt Emmanuel Biblis. Biblis, a graduate of the officer cadet school, had escaped to the Middle East after the Battle of Crete. Having received specialist training, he returned to Crete to work for the British. Biblis was based near Malathiros and regularly went to Canea to collect information.

On 17 July 1944, Biblis set off for Canea on the bus and was spotted by Major Papayannakis when a stop was made at the coast. Papayannakis, who incorrectly suspected Biblis of being a member of EAM, pointed him out to two of his men, who boarded the bus that Biblis was taking to Canea. When Biblis got off the bus the two Papayannaii followed him for some distance and, as he turned into a side street, called upon him to halt. Instead of obeying their order, Biblis pulled out a pistol and was shot dead.

After consultations with his superiors in the Middle East, Captain Ciclitira received instructions to order Papayannakis to disband his men and accept an offer of safe conduct to Cairo. Papayannakis declined the suggestion that he leave Crete.

The next encounter between ELAS and the Papayannaii took place at Palea Roumata in July 1944. Surrounded by mountains, Palea Roumata was one of the villages regularly used as a safe haven by ELAS guerrillas. The Papayannaii planned a raid on Palea Roumata but news of their plans was leaked to ELAS. Early on the morning of the proposed foray, an ambush was prepared on the approach road to the west of the village.

As a lorry crammed with Papayannaii approached, the guerrillas opened fire from both sides of the road. The gendarmes jumped from their lorry and took cover but within a few minutes realised their position was hopeless and surrendered. Four of them had been slightly wounded and were given first aid. The twenty gendarmes were taken to a nearby streambed where they spent the rest of the day being interrogated and lectured by the ELAS leaders. Just before darkness fell they were allowed to leave and made their way, barefoot, back to Voukolies.

Shortly after this ambush most of the Papayannaii deserted and the unit effectively ceased operations, although a few of the gendarmes remained loyal to their leader and continued to guard his home in his native village of Kria Vrissi, where Papayannakis occasionally spent the night. In early August 1944, ELAS guerrillas attacked and captured Papayannakis' home after a brief battle. All the gendarmes managed to make their escape except for the sergeant who had been in charge of the defenders. The sergeant was from the mainland and showed no remorse when questioned about his collaboration with the Germans. After sacking Papayannakis' home the guerrillas moved off to the mountains, taking the sergeant with them.

The following day, the sergeant was tried as a traitor, found guilty and executed. His body was thrown down a pothole but no announcement of his execution was made. A week later Papayannakis issued a warning in the local paper that if the sergeant were not returned alive he would order the execution of 100 prisoners in Agia prison. This threat was never carried out.

With liberation seemingly imminent, scores of Cretans were slipping away from their villages each night to join the guerrillas. Recruits walked for hours to reach the assembly points. As they drew near to their destination they sang resistance songs and fired their guns into the air. The newcomers were formed into companies and the local priest blessed their weapons. All who joined ELAS took an oath that they would remain loyal until their country was rid of the occupation forces. When the enrolment ceremonies were completed, the men were moved off to other bases in the hills.

As the guerrillas increased in numbers and confidence, clashes began to break out with growing frequency and the German patrols in the countryside met with escalating resistance.

An attempt to eradicate ELAS guerrillas based above Therisso ended in failure when the Germans were ambushed and forced to retreat with their casualties. In another ambush just south of Floria, seven German vehicles were destroyed and their crews killed or captured. A few days later, ELAS guerrillas lay in wait for a column of ten vehicles nearing Topolia but failed to achieve the element of surprise. A German officer was killed in the shooting but the guerrillas came under heavy fire and withdrew.

In reprisal for these attacks, hundreds of Germans surrounded Palea Roumata early one morning in the middle of August. News of the Germans' arrival preceded them and many villagers were able to flee in good time but fifteen men caught in the village were killed and several others, including the village priest, were taken hostage. Some of the houses were burnt and the locals' flocks taken away. The Germans then proceeded to Kakopetros where they executed thirty-five males. Moving on to Malathiros, they rounded up sixty-one males between the ages of thirteen and sixty-six. The prisoners were taken into the nearby gorge and shot.

Despite the reprisals the guerrillas continued their struggle. At the end of the month, a small German column was ambushed on a mountain path above Lakki as it was on its way to re-supply the garrison on the Omalos Plateau. On the following day the Germans withdrew their thirty men from the Omalos outpost.

By the middle of September, all German troops in small outlying posts in eastern Crete had been pulled back to their main bases. By 21 September the prefecture of Lasithi and the whole of the south coast of the island were free of the occupying forces.

From Heraklion many of the troops were flown to Athens at night, but the flights were intermittent as Athens airfield was being heavily bombed each day by the RAF. With the area around Heraklion under German control contracting daily, the various resistance groups began to surround the town, approaching to within a few kilometres of its walls.

Manoli Bandouvas had returned from Egypt two weeks earlier and was with his men to the east of the town. Also to the east, near the airfield, was Lt Colonel Plevres with a contingent of EOK. ELAS forces led by Yanni Podias took up position to the south of the town. The road to the west was left open.

The number of Germans inside Heraklion was estimated to be at least 1,200 and, although outnumbered by the guerrillas, they were better armed. They were also well equipped with artillery, and were capable of much death and destruction if forced to give battle. The guerrillas had little choice but to put aside all thought of offensive action and to await the German evacuation.

As the Germans began to leave town the rival groups of guerrillas forgot their political differences and began wild celebrations. Fears that reprisals would be taken on suspected collaborators with innocent people killed in the confusion began to fade as the Cretans sang songs, threw flowers, embraced each other and fired shots into the air.

But the peace was not to last. A few days later, at an official meeting of guerrilla leaders who had come together to celebrate the liberation of Heraklion, Yanni Podias was shot from behind as he stood alongside the other commanders. Athanasios Bourdzalis, who had previously assisted the British officers on the island, had taken the opportunity to settle a personal score with Podias. As rumour spread that Podias had been critically wounded and that the motive behind the shooting had been political, rioting broke out in every part of the town.

Manoli Bandouvas took the initiative and ordered his brother Nikolaos to seize Bourdzalis. The would-be assassin was arrested and given a brief trial. There was general agreement among the various guerrilla leaders that Bourdzalis should be shot to avert civil strife. The execution was carried out and peace was gradually restored to the town. Podias made a swift recovery and left for Athens.

Major Alexander Rendel, the most senior British officer in eastern Crete, had arrived on the island just after the Italian armistice and had been living in the mountains of Lasithi for a year. As the day of the impending German evacuation drew near he slipped into Heraklion and was hidden by the brother of one of his guides in a house near the harbour.

Soon after witnessing the German withdrawal from town, Rendel set off on a long tour of Lasithi to join in the celebrations with those who had hidden him. To his surprise, he discovered that ELAS was in control almost everywhere. He arrived unannounced in Neapolis one afternoon to find ELAS running the town and the bishop under house arrest for preaching anti-communist sermons. He drove on to Agios Nikolaos and again found ELAS in charge and all their political opponents in jail. ELAS leaders everywhere were eager to be seen in his company, hoping to give the local population the impression that the representative of the British government gave them his approval. In Ierapetra, Rendel was met by a vast crowd of cheering ELAS supporters and it was only in Sitia that he found EOK leaders in positions of influence. At the end of his tour, Rendel came to the conclusion that ELAS had taken over almost the entire prefecture without a shot being fired.

On the night of 15 September 1944, the leaders of EAM-ELAS and EOK agreed to meet at Tromarissa spring, high in the mountains above Zourva. Nikos Skoulas led the EOK delegation and Mitsos Vlandas represented EAM. Vlandas had recently returned to Crete to take over the leadership of EAM from Nikos Manousakis, who was seriously ill with TB.

At Tromarissa it was agreed that a committee be established, made up of an equal number of members from EOK and EAM, to manage the liberation struggle in the prefecture, oversee the smooth transition to liberation and guarantee the maintenance of law and order. ELAS and EOK guerrillas would carry out combined operations against the enemy until the liberation of the whole of Crete had been achieved.

The guerrillas were outnumbered three to one by the better-equipped German forces on the island, but, undeterred, on 25 September 1944, a Joint HQ for EAM-ELAS and EOK was established at Panagia, provocatively close to the German lines. It was not long before a clash inevitably took place.

In the late afternoon of 27 September, five ELAS guerrillas were taking mules laden with supplies to the camp at Panagia. As they approached Aletrouvari, a patrol of three Germans suddenly emerged from an olive grove a few metres ahead of them. Shooting broke out and local villagers ran to the help of the guerrillas. One German was killed and another was taken prisoner, but the third escaped into dense undergrowth and made his way back to his post at Malaxa.

From the middle of October, the new German perimeter on the island ran from Kolimbari to Georgioupolis and inland a few kilometres to the foothills of the mountains. The Germans still held control of Maleme airfield and Souda Bay but withdrawal by air and sea was now out of the question.

By the end of October 1944, the German forces on the mainland had completed their retreat from Greece, abandoning the 9,000 Germans and 5,000 Italians left in Crete to their fate. This well-armed force refused all calls to surrender and instead made plans to hold out inside Fortress Canea, where strict enforcement of the law was imposed. Roadblocks were set up and a new curfew announced: anybody found on the streets in town between 10 pm and 5 am would be arrested. No citizen was permitted to spend a night at any house except his own and nobody who was resident in the countryside could remain in town after 4 pm. Propaganda was circulated warning that a German defeat would be a victory for the Bolsheviks.

With the guerrilla forces so close to Canea, the German commander, General Hans Benthag, made plans for a major assault on their HQ. His aim was to scatter the guerrillas and to intimidate the population, and he was later to claim that the attack on Panagia was necessary to protect the town from an onslaught by the communists who, he insisted, were planning to capture Canea before the arrival of winter.

At 5.30 am on Sunday 12 November, the Germans began their attack at various points along a 15-kilometre front. The guerrillas had no artillery or mortars and only a few heavy machine guns but were determined to stand their ground.

As the Germans approached Agios Georgios the inhabitants fled and could only watch from a distance as their village was burnt. From Agios Georgios the Germans moved on towards Panagia but were pinned down by stiff resistance put up by ELAS snipers outside the village.

Elsewhere, a German company was ambushed as it ascended a path from Nerokouros to Aletrouvari. Unable to advance, the Germans exchanged fire with the guerrillas until the early evening when they withdrew to their lines.

To the east, two German platoons arrived at Stilos by truck and ordered the village president to provide them with guides to lead them to Kambi. They marched unopposed up the track from Stilos to Samonas but some ELAS reservists, who had spent a cold night sleeping out of doors, heard the approaching Germans and fired shots into the air as a warning. The Germans killed two villagers in Samonas and proceeded to Kambi. However, a runner from Samonas had already reached Kambi and alerted the villagers by ringing the church bells. The villagers took up their guns, collected on a nearby hill and prepared for battle. A few houses in the village were burnt but the Germans met such strong resistance that they were eventually compelled to withdraw.

The main German attack was spearheaded by tanks and armoured cars from Malaxa. Huge boulders had been used to block the road and hundreds of guerrillas were positioned on the higher ground to prevent the German advance. Eventually, after heavy fighting, the Germans managed to break through to Katohori and Gerolakkos, where several houses were destroyed, but were unable to make further headway.

When darkness fell, the Germans withdrew, having failed to achieve their objective of capturing Panagia. During the course of the day's battle the guerrilla HQ had been moved from Panagia to a cave a kilometre south of the village but, as their base remained unscathed, ELAS claimed a victory.

The Eagles of Crete

Throughout the following morning all was quiet but later that afternoon every piece of German artillery within range opened fire on Panagia and the surrounding villages, causing great destruction but few deaths.

In an attack just before dawn the next day, the Germans retook Agios Georgios and despite fierce resistance captured Panagia by midday, driving the guerrillas into the hills. With Panagia in flames, they advanced on Loulos, which they destroyed before withdrawing.

Despite their setbacks the Germans had, after three days, finally achieved their objective of destroying Panagia and forcing the guerrillas further back into the hills. The civilian population suffered heavily: around two hundred houses in eight villages had been destroyed, leaving approximately a thousand villagers homeless for the coming winter. A week after the battle for Panagia, ELAS moved its HQ to the more remote village of Therisso, several kilometres further to the south.

British troops entered Athens on 13 October 1944 and within a week Prime Minister George Papandreou was installed in office. On 7 November, Papandreou announced that there was no longer any need for bands of armed guerrillas to roam the countryside as the Germans, with the exception of a few scattered garrisons in Crete, Rhodes and some of the smaller islands, had withdrawn from the country completely. However, when the Greek government signed a decree dissolving all guerrilla armies ELAS refused to disband.

On Sunday 3 December, the police opened fire on a large crowd of demonstrators shouting anti-government and anti-monarchist slogans in the centre of Athens. Many were killed and wounded.

Within two days fighting had broken out between ELAS and the police throughout Athens and Piraeus. Fighting in the city escalated as ELAS took control of most of the capital and instituted a reign of terror. Hundreds of nationalists, especially those in the middle class districts, were executed and hundreds of hostages were marched off to the mountains, where many of them died from exposure.

British troops were ordered to assist the Greek government and gradually ELAS began to lose its grip on Athens. At a conference of all

Greek political parties, which began on Boxing Day, it was agreed that General Nikolaos Plastiras, a staunch republican who had been living in exile in France since his involvement in the anti-monarchist rebellion of 1935, be appointed prime minister. EAM and ELAS approved the choice of Plastiras, who took office on 3 January, and a cease-fire was agreed. Hostilities officially came to an end on 15 January.

A political settlement was ratified at Varkiza, just outside Athens, on 12 February 1945. The King agreed that he would not return to Greece until after a plebiscite on the monarchy had been held. ELAS weapons were to be handed over at specified collection points, after which ELAS would be demobilised. A new National Army was to be formed of all citizens, including former members of ELAS.

The Varkiza Agreement met many of the demands that had been made by EAM. Freedom of the press and freedom of expression were guaranteed to all citizens; trade unions were to be re-established; a purge of the civil service and gendarmerie was promised; and an amnesty was granted to all those who had committed political crimes during the fighting in Athens. However, those who refused to surrender their weapons would be unable to claim amnesty and any member of ELAS who had committed common-law crimes was to face trial.

As there was still a strong German garrison in Fortress Canea, the ELAS forces in Crete were permitted to retain their weapons.

Nobody imagined that fighting would break out among the Cretans.

Chapter 3
Civil War Looms

As on the mainland, support for ELAS in Crete was in decline and even some of the most senior officers publicly proclaimed their loyalty to the Athens government. Among these was the commander of the ELAS Regiment in Rethymnon, Lt Colonel Christos Phiotakis, who, following a meeting with representatives of the new administration, abandoned his men and left for Heraklion.

The ELAS Regiment in Rethymnon was disbanded by force soon after Phiotakis' departure by the recently appointed garrison commander of the town, Lt Colonel Pavlos Gyparis. As a young man, Gyparis had volunteered to fight the Turks in Macedonia in 1904 but, as a staunch republican, had been dismissed from the army following the failed coup attempt in 1935. Gyparis was recalled to the army just before the German invasion and served on the mainland. He was fortunate to make his getaway to Crete in a cargo ship and after the Battle of Crete he escaped to the Middle East. In January 1945, at the age of sixty-three, he was appointed garrison commander of Rethymnon.

The incident that sparked off the trouble in Rethymnon was the arrest, on 17 January, of Achilles Simitsi, a young man accused of daubing communist slogans on the town's walls. Two representatives from EAM went to see Gyparis and asked that Simitsi be released to spend the night at home. Gyparis agreed to release Simitsi on their guarantee that he present himself in court the following day.

The next morning Simitsi did not turn up in court and Gyparis gave orders for the arrest of the two EAM representatives who had guaranteed his appearance. News of the arrests spread through the town and George Sbokos, a local ELAS leader, stormed into Gyparis' office to protest at their detention. Before the war Sbokos had trained as a lawyer and had served time in Acronauplia prison for his KKE sympathies. Sbokos is said to have become abusive and threatened

Gyparis, who ordered that he be disarmed and arrested. A rumour quickly spread among members of ELAS that Sbokos had been hit on the head in a scuffle with the gendarmes and had been jailed so that nobody would see the extent of his injuries.

Anticipating trouble, Gyparis mustered a large force of nationalists and marched on the town's Venetian fortress, which, since the retreat of the Germans from the town, had been garrisoned jointly by ELAS and EOK. Gyparis disarmed the small ELAS unit and sent the men home with orders to stay indoors. The captured ELAS weapons were given to local nationalists.

Later that morning armed ELAS guerrillas took over two or three buildings in town and demanded the release of the three men who had been arrested. They were given until 4 pm to disperse but when the deadline came and went with no sign of ELAS giving way, Gyparis ordered his men to clear the town of the guerrillas. Six guerrillas were killed in the fighting and ELAS withdrew to the countryside.

The guerrillas took up positions on the heights outside town. Little attempt was made by either side at negotiation. Gyparis launched an attack on ELAS and captured their positions in less than an hour. Several guerrillas were killed in the engagement; on Gyparis' side, the only man to lose his life was Gyparis' nephew, Emmanuel.

The ELAS guerrillas retreated to Tria Monastiria and by the following day around 100 guerrillas had assembled in their new stronghold. Gyparis arrived with an equal number of gendarmes and volunteers and a fierce battle took place. Eventually the guerrillas gave way and made off in the direction of Canea. Gyparis' men marched overnight in a snowstorm and attacked the ELAS forces near Mathes, killing the ELAS leaders. The remaining guerrillas scattered into the hills or returned to their homes.

In Rethymnon, Gyparis gave members of ELAS and their supporters in the town one week to surrender their arms. By Gyparis' deadline, the guerrillas had handed over four mortars, two dozen machine guns and hundreds of rifles. Twenty-seven men had died in the three days of fighting but in the years of strife that followed in Crete, Rethymnon was to remain relatively peaceful.

The Eagles of Crete

A few days after the fighting in Rethymnon, hostilities broke out in Heraklion between a unit of ELAS and members of Bandouvas' band. Bandouvas had been working closely with Colonel Plevres since the liberation of the island and their combined forces were superior in arms and numbers to ELAS. In the brief skirmishes in Heraklion six ELAS guerrillas were killed and their comrades swiftly driven out of town. Bandouvas' men suffered no losses but two British soldiers lost their lives, shot by ELAS snipers when their jeep came under fire. ELAS guerrillas were ordered to disarm without delay, and although few weapons were handed in, there was every indication that ELAS was a spent force in the prefecture.

In Lasithi, the initial post-liberation enthusiasm for ELAS that Major Rendel had witnessed was rapidly disappearing. With news of the bloodshed in Athens, the selection of Plastiras as prime minister, and the three months of complete freedom since the Germans had left the area, many members of ELAS abandoned the organisation. Most of their leaders did the same, and by early February, ELAS had ceased to have any significant influence in the east of the island.

The ELAS leadership in Canea prefecture watched events in the rest of Crete with some apprehension. Fearing that Gyparis would move to attack them, ELAS reservists seized the strategic pass at Klima, in the mountains on the Canea/Rethymnon border.

The morning after their seizure of Klima, a small band of EOK nationalists arrived at the pass on their way from Canea to Rethymnon. ELAS held Klima in force and turned them back. In anger, the nationalists attacked Ramni, an ELAS stronghold, but were themselves attacked by a large band of ELAS guerrillas camped nearby. There was a brief fight, in which one of the nationalists was killed and the rest were surrounded and taken prisoner. The nationalists were later released after being disarmed.

Trouble between ELAS and EOK in Apokoronas, the north-eastern province of Canea, began to spread as both sides seized hostages. With the intention of moving into Canea prefecture and assisting their comrades, a band of nationalists from Asi Gonia set out for Klima. It was a warm day and as they approached the pass they noticed that the sentry on duty had taken off his clothes and was busy delousing them in the winter sunshine. The nationalists had no difficulty in capturing him but another guerrilla, who had spotted them from a distance, sounded the alarm and ELAS reinforcements appeared in time to block their way.

With a powerful German force still present on the island, both sides were anxious to avoid conflict. Talks were held, and on 3 February a treaty was signed between EAM-ELAS and EOK in Fres. All hostages were released and it was agreed that a mixed garrison of ELAS and EOK, made up of five soldiers and one officer from each organisation, should guard Klima. This garrison was to guarantee freedom of movement between the prefectures of Rethymnon and Canea for individuals who had legitimate reasons of travel between the two areas. Passage to all bands of armed men would be refused.

On 4 March, from his headquarters in Therisso, Colonel Gregory Kondekakis, the commander of ELAS forces on Crete, gave the official order for ELAS guerrillas to disband in the parts of the island that had been liberated. Only the ELAS Regiment in Canea was to be retained, fully armed, until the German surrender.

Despite the treaty signed between the leaders of ELAS and EOK at Fres, tension between the extremists of the two sides persisted. On 25 March, Greek Independence Day, a festival took place in Fres and early that morning a large crowd arrived from neighbouring villages and joined the hundreds of villagers already in the square.

As soon as the church service ended, local musicians began to entertain the crowd. The music had only just started when a large group of nationalists began to fire shots in the air and taunt the ELASites who were present. By chance, a stray bullet wounded a former ELAS platoon commander and fighting erupted. The nationalists were driven out of the village but they reassembled on a nearby hill. As soon as armed nationalists arrived from Tzitzifes they returned to the attack on ELAS. One ELAS guerrilla was shot and killed in the second round of fighting and both sides withdrew as darkness fell.

The Eagles of Crete

The conflict continued the following day and spread to nearby villages. When news of the fighting reached Gyparis he mobilised 300 men and set out for Fres. Gyparis, with his overwhelming superiority was in no mood to negotiate and hostilities continued until ELAS was defeated. Fifteen men died in the fighting, bringing the total of those killed in the civil conflict that had started in Crete two months earlier to fifty.

On 7 May the end of the war with Germany was announced. As the news spread, people ran into the streets to celebrate. Hundreds flocked to the seafront in Canea; a large Greek flag was produced and singing broke out among the jubilant citizens. Local party politics were forgotten as everybody united to rejoice that the occupation was over and the day of liberation had finally arrived. German posters were torn down and frenziedly trampled underfoot. Crowds of singing and chanting Cretans began to make their way to the harbour from every direction.

Fearing that the situation might get out of hand, the heavily armed German police alerted Bishop Xirouhakis, who they had used as a mediator in the past. The bishop rushed to the harbour and begged the crowd to avoid provoking the Germans and return quietly to their homes. Gradually people began to disperse and by the time the curfew came into force the streets were empty.

On 9 May, General Hans Benthag signed an agreement surrendering power in Canea. German troops were allowed to keep their side arms for their personal protection and began to evacuate the town and move to the Akrotiri, where newly-arrived British troops put a cordon across the neck of the peninsula. Before withdrawing from their positions, the Germans fired all their artillery shells out to sea. An announcement was made to the general population that it was futile to collect German weapons as all the arms factories in Germany had been destroyed and no spare parts or ammunition would be available in the future. This did not stop the Cretans from bartering with the Germans for their weapons.

The official entrance of Greek forces into Canea took place on 23 May. Leading the parade were Lt Colonel Gyparis and Manoli Bandouvas, followed by around 300 of their men. A battalion of the new National Army followed. It had been agreed beforehand that ELAS would not take part in the procession.

The column marched through the main streets of the town to the cheers of the crowds standing on the pavements. Flowers were strewn everywhere and Greek flags fluttered from the balconies. At Dikastirion Square, the procession came to a halt in front of Bishop Xirouhakis and other dignitaries. There followed a short ceremony in which the bishop handed over the town to the commander of the National Army.

The ceremony over, all the troops marched to the town barracks. They were accompanied by a mass of spectators, many of whom, still chanting and cheering, followed the parade through the entrance to the army camp. Without warning, those who had entered the camp were attacked by up to twenty of Gyparis' men who struck them with rifle butts and screamed at them to leave the barracks. There were so many people behind them that it was difficult for those inside to withdraw, and before they could do so more of Gyparis' men appeared at the windows of the upper floor of the barracks and fired shots into the crowd on the road.

Panic broke out as people tried to make a run for it. Many were trampled in the crush and a woman was shot and killed. Peace was restored when a British officer ordered one of his men to fire a burst from a machine gun, aimed at just below the windows that Gyparis' men were using.

Yanni Manousakas was a sandal-maker by trade. Born in 1907 in the prefecture of Rethymnon, he was elected president of his village, Agios Konstantinos, at the age of twenty-six. He was soon busy organising secret KKE cells, an occupation he carried out successfully for three years until his arrest and imprisonment in 1936.

Manousakas spent several years in the Acronauplia prison before being transferred in 1943 to Corfu prison, in the Italian zone. When the Italian government capitulated later that year all prisoners on the island were suddenly released. For a short while they remained at liberty on Corfu but when rumours spread that the Germans were on their way to take control of the island they fled to the mainland. With several others, Manousakas made his way to the Pindus Mountains where he joined up with ELAS. For the final months of the occupation he received training as an officer and served near Larissa.

Following the liberation, Manousakas was employed in the Larissa area by the KKE but later that summer was informed that he was going to be sent to work for the Party in Crete. Manousakas was eager to return to Crete; he had been away for nine years.

On arrival in Canea, Manousakas met up with Mitsos Vlandas, who arranged for his appointment to the KKE committee in Rethymnon to fill a vacancy created by a member who had fled to his village after the fighting in January. Manousakas was provided with a sum of money and the names of reliable contacts in the prefecture.

Before starting work, Manousakas paid a brief visit to his family and old friends in his village. His younger brother had been killed in action on the Albanian front and his father had died during the occupation but Manousakas found his mother and several of his brothers and sisters at home. At the large family gathering on the evening of his arrival, his mother produced a bottle of red wine that she had put aside in the year of his arrest to keep for his return.

In Athens, at the end of January 1946, an announcement was made that a general election would be held on 31 March. As law and order in the countryside throughout the mainland continued to deteriorate, EAM leaders in Athens requested a two month postponement to the elections. They demanded that all right-wing bands should be disarmed; the army and civil service purged of former collaborators; and persecution of former members of EAM-ELAS should cease. In the previous twelve months they claimed that a total of 25,000 arrests had been made. Of these, only a few dozen had been arrested for collaboration with the Germans; the remainder were all members and supporters of EAM-ELAS.

As none of their demands were met, the KKE leaders announced on 22 February that they would not participate in the elections and called on their supporters to boycott them.

The elections went ahead as planned and the outright winner was the pro-royalist United National Front Party, led by Constantine Tsaldaris, which won 55% of the vote and 206 of the 350 seats. The number of those who had boycotted the elections for political reasons was officially put at around 10%.

The March 1946 elections in Crete passed off without incident. KKE members observed the call to boycott proceedings and the Communist Party later insisted that the 30% of the electorate in Crete who failed to vote were all communists supporting the Party's appeal for a boycott.

In Canea in early May, there was a large gathering of the KKE leadership, which was attended by around three dozen representatives from all over the island. Those taking part in the proceedings were not to know it, but this was to be the last legal meeting of the KKE leadership in Crete for almost thirty years.

In the election of officials for the Cretan regional committee of the KKE, Dimitri Vlandas was re-appointed first secretary and Yanni Manousakas was elected to the central committee and given the job of organising self-defence units of former ELAS men in the event of attack from their political enemies. It was agreed to hide two printing presses - one in Canea and the other in Heraklion – with a sufficient supply of paper and ink.

Vlandas was recalled to the mainland in July and his replacement was 40-year-old George Tsitilos, who had worked for EAM in the Peloponnese during the occupation and had been employed on the staff of the *Rizospastis* newspaper. Tsitilos had studied mathematics at Athens University but had been expelled for taking part in student strikes. On liberation he had married Toula, a member of EPON. The pair arrived from Athens with their baby daughter as Vlandas departed.

Shortly after the elections of 1946, a law was passed reintroducing the death penalty for illegal possession of weapons and for membership of armed bands. Another law prohibiting strikes swiftly followed. The police were given powers of search and arrest without warrant, and the collecting of donations or subscriptions for political parties was made illegal. In July, a bill proposing that the families of army deserters should be deported to remote islands was passed into law.

There was to be a referendum on the monarchy on 1 September and expectations that the Cretans would vote for a republic were high. At a rally in Heraklion, Manoli Bandouvas shared a platform with the communists and appealed to a crowd of 15,000 for unity among the Cretans and a vote for a republic. In Canea, General Mandakas addressed a crowd in the Olympia cinema, warning his listeners that the choice they faced in the plebiscite was between monarchy and democracy. He urged his audience to vote for the latter in the form of a republic.

In a crowded *kapheneion* in a suburb of Canea one evening, two gendarmes tried unsuccessfully to tear down anti-monarchist posters. The gendarmes threatened and swore at the customers and as more people crowded into the *kapheneion* to see what was happening they took out their pistols and fired into the air. There were no casualties and the gendarmes hurriedly withdrew.

When the plebiscite was held, the overall result throughout the country was a resounding 70% in favour of the return of King George II. It was only in Salonika, Piraeus and Crete that a majority of votes favoured a republic. In Crete, the national percentages were reversed with just 30% voting for a return of the monarch. Leading articles in the *Dimokratia*, the EAM newspaper in Canea, complained bitterly that electoral fraud had taken place on the mainland. The editor of the *Dimokratia* was arrested the day after the plebiscite and charged under an ancient law with insulting the monarchy.

Two days after the plebiscite, martial law was proclaimed in northern Greece and a roundup began of former ELAS officers, who were exiled to remote islands without trial. However, attempts by the authorities to detain some of the leading communists in Crete came to nothing. George Sbokos was arrested and accused of holding an illegal gathering but was released after protests from his influential friends.

As soon as he was set free, Sbokos made for Mount Ida, where he began to organise an armed band. Yanni Manousakas spent two nights in jail for attempting to organise a public meeting in Canea but charges were dropped and he was released.

Towards the end of September, police in Canea burst into the home of Vangelio Kladou and arrested her and her guests. Kladou was the only female member of the central committee of the KKE in Crete and was entertaining three guests that day, one of whom was George Tsitilos.

Born in 1920, Kladou was from Anogia, the daughter of a postal clerk, and showed such potential at school that her relatives provided her with financial help to go to Athens to study to become a teacher. It was in Athens that she came into contact with communist literature and ideas and, in 1940, joined the KKE. In September 1940 she was appointed as schoolteacher in the mountain village of Miriokefala. After the Battle of Crete, she helped to hide Allied soldiers who passed through the village on their way to the south coast to seek passage to the Middle East. Kladou joined EPON on its formation and when she was transferred to a larger school at Episkopi she became a courier for the resistance. As the Germans retreated from Rethymnon, she led an armed band of young guerrillas into the town.

Lawyers went to the police station to request an explanation for the arrest of Kladou and her friends and demand to know what charges their clients were to face. No explanation was forthcoming and requests to meet with the provincial governor fell on deaf ears.

However, five days after they were arrested, Kladou and her guests were released without charge. The police issued a statement explaining that they had searched Kladou's home in the hunt for a wanted criminal who was believed to be hiding there. As it was clear that Kladou and her guests knew nothing of the fugitive, they were being released, although a large amount of cash found in the house would be confiscated as it was believed to be money that had been collected illegally on behalf of the KKE.

Shortly after the release of Kladou and her friends it was the turn of Nikos Kokovlis to be taken into custody. Born into a prosperous farming family in Asia Minor, Kokovlis was only two years old when his family was forced to flee and join the flood of refugees attempting to escape the advancing Turkish army. Almost everything they had worked so hard for all their lives was abandoned as the refugees took with them what little they could carry on their backs or load into their few ox-carts. The Kokovlis family made it to the coast where a boat took them to safety in Samos. Following the treaty which confirmed the permanent exchange of populations between Greece and Turkey, the Kokovlis family was given property in Vamvakopoulo, just outside Canea, which had until then been owned by Cretan-born Turks.

Kokovlis was studying in Athens when war broke out with the Italians. Rejected by the Greek army when he tried to volunteer for service on the front, Kokovlis was in Athens on the day the German army marched into the capital. Not long afterwards, he set sail for Canea in a rusty old caique with some Cretan soldiers from the Albanian front. On arrival in Canea the men were arrested and forced to work for the Germans, loading and unloading trucks. A short time later, Kokovlis disappeared. He spent the years of the occupation working for EAM in Canea.

Soon after the end of the war, Kokovlis was one of six KKE members chosen to represent Canea at the Party's Pan-Cretan Conference. Shortly afterwards, at the age of twenty-six, he was elected Secretary of the Canea Workers' Centre.

On the afternoon of 13 November 1946, Kokovlis was alone in his office when half a dozen policemen walked in and asked him to go with them. He demanded to see their warrant but was seized, taken outside and thrown into a car. Kokovlis was driven to the police station and pushed into a small, filthy, windowless cell where he was kept in isolation.

News of Kokovlis' arrest spread quickly and delegations of union leaders and workers arrived at the police station to protest at his detention. The police announced that they intended to charge Kokovlis with involvement in the murder of a gendarme major who had been assassinated in Canea in February 1945. A few days after the killing, the KKE had issued a proclamation stating that the gendarme had been executed because he had handed over patriots to the Germans. Kokovlis was kept in prison for four days and then, as suddenly as he had been arrested, was released without charge.

One large gathering the police made no attempt to prevent was the rally held for two hours in the Olympia cinema on 24 November 1946 to celebrate the twenty-eighth anniversary of the founding of the KKE. The cinema was adorned with red flags and a minute's silence for those who had died in the war was observed before the start of proceedings. The main speaker was George Tsitilos, who detailed the struggle that had taken place to establish the KKE and reminded his audience of the improvements that workers had enjoyed in their lives since the founding of the Party. To loud cheers from his packed audience, he demanded that the KKE should be allowed to take part in the government of the country. Everybody joined in singing ELAS resistance songs and the National Anthem before the huge crowd left peacefully.

A special court had been set up in Canea after the liberation to try those accused of collaborating with the Germans. A few who had grown rich from the black market were also brought before this court to answer for their conduct. In all, around 60 people were found guilty. Four were given the death penalty. Another four were sentenced to life imprisonment and the rest were given sentences ranging from eight months to twenty years.

Major Dimitri Papayannakis, commander of the Special Gendarme Battalion that had been raised by the Germans to fight ELAS, was the most senior defendant to appear before the court. Papayannakis was charged with working for the enemy and of being directly involved in the murder of Emmanuel Biblis, the British agent who had been killed by two of his gendarmes. His trial was to last for three weeks.

The first witness for the prosecution was Nikos Biblis, the murdered agent's father. Biblis told the court that there was no doubt in his mind that Papayannakis had given the order for his son's murder. A clerk who had been employed by the Germans also provided evidence

The Eagles of Crete

against Papayannakis. Among others testifying against the major were a doctor and two of his former gendarmes. In his defence, Papayannakis offered a doctor, a lawyer and a gendarme sergeant major as witnesses. All three of these men gave evidence that Papayannakis had set up his gendarme battalion with the full knowledge of the British officers on the island and that the major was a true patriot who had done no harm to his country during the occupation.

Papayannakis was found not guilty and the court expressed doubt that he had consciously become a German agent. There was a lack of evidence that the major had provided the Germans with any useful information and no proof that he had personally given the order for Biblis' murder. Papayannakis was released, but so great was the public outrage at the court's decision that family and friends persuaded him to leave Crete and move to Athens.

After a few months, Papayannakis tired of life in the capital and decided to return to Crete, where he walked the streets quite openly. Early one Saturday evening, towards the end of October 1946, Papayannakis was standing at the entrance to a jewellery shop belonging to his friend, Yanni Kriaris. As the two men chatted, they took no notice as a young man came along the street towards the shop. When the young man drew level with them, he pulled out a pistol, fired three shots into Papayannakis' body and made off into the surrounding network of narrow streets. Papayannakis was taken to hospital, where he died of his wounds later that evening.

The assassin was never found. Everything had happened very quickly and Kriaris had not had a close look at the young man. He was able to tell the police that the suspect was of medium height and weight, but no other eyewitnesses came forward and although the police arrested a young communist suspect they were forced to release him for lack of evidence.

None of the rank and file gendarmes who had served under Papayannakis were ever brought before a court, unlike members of Schubert's unit who were arrested on sight. The Schuberai were tried for collaboration and murder in Heraklion and Athens and without exception all were found guilty and executed. In one case, a small group of collaborators awaiting trial in Heraklion was attacked and slain by a mob, saving the formality of a trial.

Fritz Schubert, the unit's leader, was captured as he attempted to re-enter Greece at the end of the war. After several postponements his trial eventually began at the end of July 1947 and he was found guilty of murder. On 22 October he was executed by firing squad. Just before the execution, the officer in charge told his men that: "The innocent souls of this criminal's victims are hovering over your weapons, waiting to direct your bullets into this butcher's heart."

Chapter 4
Fighting in the East

In August 1946 a KKE official was murdered outside his home in Perivolia and a few weeks later, in Neo Horio, a member of EPON was shot dead late at night as he was crossing the village square. In retaliation, the village priest of Neo Horio was shot in the chest as he made his way home one evening after visiting relatives. A prominent nationalist, the 45-year-old priest died of his wounds before a doctor could arrive.

The morning after the priest was killed, the police searched the EAM offices in Canea, claiming to be looking for a wanted man. No wanted man was found but, carefully hidden away, the police discovered nine Italian hand grenades. A few days later the EPON offices were broken into during the night. Documents were taken, furniture was smashed up, pictures of Stalin were torn down and a fire was started by the intruders as they left the building.

With the political climate so unsettled, Yanni Manousakas travelled around the island selecting men to lead bands of guerrillas, which would be united under his leadership in a force he proudly referred to as The Democratic Army of Crete. Many experienced officers who had served with ELAS were willing to help him.

In Canea, the men chosen by Manousakas to be his senior *kapetans* were Mihali Papapanayiotakis (known as *Kapetan* Mihali), and Nikos Tsamantis. *Kapetan* Mihali was serving as an officer with an infantry regiment near Olympus when the Germans invaded Greece. Wounded in the retreat, he took to the mountains on the formation of ELAS, rising to the rank of colonel by the end of the war. When the war ended he returned to Crete and for a brief period was an assistant bank manager. Nikos Tsamantis had proved himself a capable ELAS *kapetan* during the occupation and had played a leading role in the destruction of Schubert's band of collaborators.

Manousakas could also rely on Yanni Bandourakis, Manoli Pissadakis and George Kodelas, all of whom were in hiding. Bandourakis had been born in Kourphalona, just outside Kastelli, and served as an ELAS *kapetan* during the occupation. Pissadakis had set up one of the first ELAS bands on the island and survived a German concentration camp. George Kodelas had been a major with ELAS in the Peloponnese during the occupation and had taken part in the Battle in Athens in December 1944. After the Varkiza Agreement he had arrived in Crete with his wife and for a short time worked openly as a butcher. When a warrant for his arrest was issued and a reward offered for his capture, he took to the mountains and assumed the *nom de guerre* of *Kapetan* George.

Manousakas was also very satisfied with the two senior men - Yanni Podias, the Heraklion ELAS commander, and Mitsos Paparaftis, who was known as *Kapetan* Papas - available to him in the prefecture of Heraklion. Paparaftis was a mainlander from Trikala in Thessaly and had been a member of the KKE since 1928. He was a skilled mechanic and on being arrested by the Germans in Piraeus in 1941 was taken to Heraklion to help them repair one of their ships lying damaged in the harbour. Instead of carrying out the necessary repairs, Paparaftis sabotaged and sank the ship single-handed before escaping to the mountains to join the guerrillas.

At the end of October, the Ministry of Public Order announced a reward of three million drachmas for the capture of Yanni Bandourakis and his close friend, Emmanuel Bikakis.

Bandourakis was wanted for murdering citizens during the occupation. Bandourakis' reply to this accusation was that if he had killed any Cretans during the occupation his victims were traitors and collaborators.

Bikakis had served with ELAS until he was drafted into the new National Army. While serving in Rethymnon, however, he got into a fight and wounded two nationalists. He deserted and fled to the mountains, later claiming that he had acted in self-defence. Both the former ELAS men faced additional charges of robbery, forming an armed band and terrorising villagers.

The Eagles of Crete

On 1 January 1947 the two men, armed with machine guns, held up a gendarme and robbed him of his pistol. A few days later a gendarme spotted Bandourakis as he sat in a *kapheneion* in Drapanias with two friends. Bandourakis realised he had been recognised and before the gendarme could summon assistance the three men made off through the olive groves.

Gendarme reinforcements arrived from Canea and took over the local school. For several days they used the school as their base, going out on patrol during the day and putting up checkpoints and setting ambushes at night. After fruitless days spent waiting for Bandourakis to fall into their trap, the gendarmes moved to Deliana.

Eventually, Bandourakis and his men were cornered and a gun battle broke out. Night began to fall and as the gendarmes made a daring assault on Bandourakis' position one of the gendarmes was shot in the head and killed instantly. Bandourakis and his men slipped away into the darkness.

Two weeks after the killing of the gendarme, twenty armed men were in action near Gavalohori following the arrest of Stamatis Alexandrakis. Alexandrakis had failed to report for duty when he received his call-up papers but on a trip to Vamos was recognised and seized by gendarmes. The young man's relatives from Ramni went to the nearest band of guerrillas to ask for their help in releasing him. It was known that Alexandrakis would be transferred from the gendarme post at Vamos to Canea the next day and it was assumed the transfer would be made by bus. An ambush site was decided on later that evening.

The Vamos bus, full of passengers, left at its usual time the following morning. As the driver slowed at a junction near Gavalohori his bus was hit by a hail of bullets. Two female passengers were wounded and the driver suffered a serious leg wound. The armed men surrounded the bus and demanded the release of Alexandrakis, only to be informed that he was still in Vamos and would be taken to Canea later that day under an escort of gendarmes. One of Alexandrakis' relatives hurriedly searched the bus and when the driver's story was confirmed they set off in haste to Ramni, using minor paths through the woodland.

At the end of January 1947 a lone gendarme was murdered near Stilos. A few days later, Pavlos Gyparis was appointed the military commander of Canea. This was an unpopular appointment among those who blamed Gyparis for precipitating the fighting in Rethymnon in which many members of ELAS had lost their lives. The government insisted that Gyparis was the best man to provide security for the island following the recent breakdown in law and order and with armed men roaming the countryside.

Gyparis immediately took a firm line against the left. When the unions announced that strikes and demonstrations for better pay and working conditions would take place in early March Gyparis banned the demonstrations and declared that he would use force to break up any large gatherings that took place. To avoid the risk of bloodshed, the unions abandoned the planned demonstrations but insisted the strikes went ahead.

Although many in the workforce were disgruntled, the strikes met with varying success. In the other three prefectures they very soon collapsed, but the roadblocks set up by the strikers to the east of Canea to prevent the movement of goods proved to be very effective and Canea was completely cut off from the rest of Crete for several days.

On the day the strikes began, Bandourakis and his men surrounded the gendarme post at Deliana, taking the garrison of eight men completely by surprise. Only the sergeant in charge offered resistance and he was shot in the stomach and mortally wounded. Having disarmed the gendarmes, Bandourakis and his men made off into the hills.

Following the attack on the gendarme post at Deliana, Gyparis announced the formation of a battalion of volunteer gendarmes under his direct command. These men would not receive the formal training that gendarmes underwent and, in effect, would be his private army. According to his enemies, Gyparis was happy to allow former criminals, sheep thieves and ex-prisoners into this special force provided that the men were anti-communist. Gyparis' volunteers, who were known as Gypari, soon became widely feared as they took the offensive in the fight to wipe out the small bands of armed men in the hills.

The Eagles of Crete

At Easter a large crowd gathered at the convent of Chrisopigi, just outside Canea. The weather was exceptionally good and many families made the short walk from town to enjoy the celebrations. The mood was cheerful and the wine flowed freely. A small group of former members of EPON began to sing political songs, much to the annoyance of some nationalists in the crowd.

The ill feeling between the two sides came to a head when the EPONites refused to stop singing. Insults were exchanged and, in an instant, knives and pistols were produced. Fighting broke out and one of the nationalists from Neo Horio was stabbed. Another was almost clubbed to death before being rescued by his friends and a third was shot and seriously wounded by a man who slipped away in the confusion. The authorities blamed the EPONites for starting the brawl and arrested six of them a few days later.

A week after the arrest of these EPONites in Canea, some of the soldiers based at the army camp in Agios Nikolaos deserted their battalion. The soldiers, many of whom were left-wingers from the mainland, had frequently debated the possibility of making their way to join the bands of armed men in Central Greece and had made contact with local KKE leaders for advice. The KKE in Crete, however, was in no position to convey a large number of fugitives to the mainland so it had been agreed that the soldiers should take to the mountains and join up with local guerrillas.

The officers in the army camp were aware that many of the men under their command were of dubious loyalty and had placed restrictions on their movements. They were quite happy, however, to allow a football match to take place late one Sunday afternoon between the battalion and a local team. The match was due to finish an hour before darkness fell and the soldiers made contact with the KKE leaders beforehand to check that arrangements had been made for their desertion. Reassured, 55 soldiers walked off into the hills in small groups as soon as the match finished. They were met by guides who took them to join Yanni Roukounakis, the local communist leader in the Dikti Mountains.

Reports that soldiers had deserted their battalion and joined up with guerrillas in eastern Crete prompted the Security Police in Canea to round up a dozen influential left-wingers that they considered a danger to society. Orders were issued, and at 3 am the following morning the police burst into the homes of the twelve men. Ten of them were arrested but two, the lawyer Vangelis Hatziangelis and union leader Nikos Kokovlis, who had taken the precaution of not sleeping at home, escaped capture.

Strikes were called in protest at the arrest of the ten men and demands were made for their immediate release. A police official confirmed rumours that the men would be sent to Piraeus and thence exiled to a remote island prison. Gyparis publicly condemned the KKE leaders for supporting the groups of armed men in the mountains and for encouraging soldiers in the armed forces to desert. A front-page leading article in the Kyrix newspaper appealed for peace but the public mood was anything but peaceful. A number of leftists went into hiding or took to the mountains rather than face possible arrest and deportation.

The arrests in Canea led to a spate of attacks in the countryside. Manoli Pissadakis and many former ELAS men had gathered at the church of St George in Drakona to celebrate the Saint's Day. When a messenger arrived with the news, forty of them set off to attack the gendarme post at Therisso. Taken completely by surprise, the officer and three gendarmes surrendered without a shot being fired and were led away as hostages, to be exchanged for the release of the ten leftists arrested in town.

Another armed band captured the gendarme post at Fres early the following morning while the sergeant and his two men were asleep. The gendarmes, their weapons and files were taken to a nearby guerrilla hide-out. At Armeni later that morning the small squad of gendarmes was tipped off that armed men were approaching. Immediately the gendarmes abandoned their post, taking their weapons and papers with them. The following day the gendarmes who had been captured at Therisso and Fres were released unharmed.

Fighting broke out between an armed band and gendarmes near Kokkino Horio, while at Plakalona more armed men set up a roadblock and stopped the traffic. All the telegraph poles in the vicinity were cut down and the road was only cleared when a gendarme patrol approached. Telegraph poles were also brought down around Floria, cutting communication with the south of the island. *Kapetan* George successfully led thirty armed men against the gendarme station at Vathi, capturing it and abducting the four men posted there.

Yanni Bandourakis led 30 men, mostly from Palea Roumata, in an attack on a small gendarme patrol near Anoskeli. A sergeant was killed in the hour-long battle and the gendarmes forced to retreat. Gendarme reinforcements that had set out for Anoskeli were ambushed by guerrillas outside Voukolies.

The following day, Bandourakis was reported to be moving towards Tavronitis from Voukolies with around 50 armed men, cutting down all the telegraph poles along their route. A mixed force of 30 gendarmes and soldiers was hurriedly dispatched from Agia by truck to reinforce Tavronitis.

The guerrillas came to a halt on the hill above the Tavronitis road and took up positions in trenches that had been dug by the Germans. When the truck carrying the troops from Agia was spotted in the distance the guerrillas waited until it started to cross the bridge over the Tavronitis. With the truck well within their range they opened fire with heavy machine guns, blowing out its tyres and bringing the vehicle to an immediate halt.

The troops leapt from the truck and took what cover they could find at the side of the road. Although pinned down and under heavy fire, several of them managed to make a run for it and escape, but twelve of them and the gendarme captain in charge of the platoon were taken prisoner. The guerrillas lost one man killed; one gendarme and one soldier were later found dead and five wounded gendarmes were left beside the broken-down truck. In the backyard of a nearby *kapheneion* the guerrillas executed the gendarme captain and then set off for the hills with their eleven prisoners.

The prisoners were released the following day but one soldier, a Macedonian doing his national service in Crete, chose to stay with the guerrillas. To the guerrillas he henceforth became known as Tavronitis.

Faced with this widespread disorder, Gyparis led a large patrol to Kissamos, meeting no resistance along his route. When he was satisfied that the guerrilla bands in the west had dispersed, he made preparations for a show of military force to the east of Canea.

For five days, fifty men had been blocking the main road to Heraklion at Neo Horio, and a heavy machine gun had been set up beside the church in the upper part of the village, overlooking the road. Pissadakis was reported to be outside Malaxa with a large number of men, using trenches and fortifications constructed by the Germans as their stronghold. Other, smaller groups of armed men had been moving around the area cutting the telephone wires and in one case, near Kalami, the engineers who were sent to repair the telephone lines were held up and forced to hand over their equipment.

At the end of the first week in May, Gyparis set off for Malaxa in a convoy of trucks carrying a hundred men. They met with no resistance on the drive up to Malaxa as Pissadakis and his band had been warned of his approach and had withdrawn. Gyparis proceeded down the new road built by the Germans to Megala Horafia and met no opposition until he was approaching Provarma, Pissadakis' native village, where shots were fired at the leading trucks. Despite putting up a fierce struggle, the guerrillas were driven slowly south and were forced to split into smaller groups. Most of the men retreated to Ramni. Gyparis continued south to Pemonia and made camp there for the night.

On the following day, Gyparis launched an attack on Ramni but met with such fierce resistance that mortars were used and it was not until the village was virtually surrounded that the guerrillas withdrew higher into the mountains. There was only one casualty: a village woman who was killed by a stray bullet.

Gyparis assembled the villagers in the square and warned them that they should not allow armed men to enter their village in future. He assured them that they would be allowed to continue working their fields in peace and nobody would bother them if they avoided involvement with the guerrillas. He then returned with his men to Pemonia for the night.

The next morning, Gyparis made a tour of the nearby villages, many of which were known to have sided with the guerrillas. In each village he stopped, assembled the inhabitants and repeated the same speech he had made at Ramni. He was openly scornful of the guerrillas, claiming they were a disorganised rabble incapable of fighting a pitched battle, and warned of serious consequences for those who joined them. He met no armed opposition and returned to town that evening. A curfew was imposed throughout the prefecture of Canea, with a penalty of three months' imprisonment for those who failed to observe it.

After the sudden outbreak of violence at the end of April a relative calm now descended on western Crete. The whole prefecture of Rethymnon was peaceful and the southern part of the Canea prefecture had remained quiet despite the outbreak of trouble in the north. Leading articles in the newspapers asserted that the left was not as strong as its supporters claimed and praised the Cretan people for not getting involved in the turmoil. Manoli Bandouvas added his voice to the appeals for peace, saying that enough Cretan blood had been shed during the German occupation and that Crete should set an example to the rest of Greece and avoid civil war.

The morning after the desertion of the 55 soldiers from Agios Nikolaos the army sent out patrols in pursuit. Yanni Roukounakis led only a dozen men but he had arranged for food and weapons to be ready for the deserters when they joined him. With his augmented band he moved slowly towards Kroustas.

It was not long before his position was located by an army patrol. Under orders not to take offensive action, the patrol followed the deserters, hoping that they would see the hopelessness of their situation and surrender. Earlier that day the military commander of the army camp at Agios Nikolaos had publicly announced that if the deserters surrendered they would suffer no punishment, and villagers were asked to pass this message on to the men, should they come into contact with them. The commander's pleas were ignored and Roukounakis led his large band southwards, losing the army patrol in the forests.

At Kalamafka, Roukounakis joined forces with Podias. The first armed action in eastern Crete had already taken place the previous day when George Sbokos had led a few armed men in an attack on the gendarme post at Mires. One gendarme was killed and the sergeant in charge of the post was wounded in the brief engagement.

With their united forces, Podias and Roukounakis made plans for an audacious attack on Ierapetra, which was garrisoned by only a small force of gendarmes. The guerrillas were in urgent need of supplies and the guerrilla leaders expected their surprise attack to meet with little opposition.

At 4 am on 9 May 1947, Podias and 100 men descended the mountain in small groups and moved into Ierapetra. Telephone wires were cut and armed men posted on street corners. Machine guns were set up on rooftops overlooking the gendarme station and when the gendarmes awoke they found themselves surrounded. Although they repulsed the fierce attack made upon them they remained besieged in their post, unable to prevent the guerrillas from taking over the town.

Once in control of Ierapetra, Podias' men broke into warehouses and carried off sacks of flour, sugar, rice and spaghetti, cases of tinned meat and blankets, all of which they loaded into two trucks. They set fire to the warehouses and then turned their attention to the shops, taking all the cigarettes and chocolate they could find.

Their attempt to steal the 265 million drachmas from the safe in the local bank was foiled when they failed to get hold of both the keys needed to open it. They captured the bank manager and took his key but it was useless without the second one, which was in the possession of the cashier, and he had gone into hiding as soon as he heard the first gunshots fired. Podias sent several runners around the town to shout a demand that the cashier surrender immediately, warning that if he failed to do so he would be shot when caught. Despite these threats the cashier remained in hiding and the guerrillas failed to break open the safe.

A group of Albanian refugees happened to be in Ierapetra, in exile because of their opposition to the communist regime in their own country. When Podias' men found them they shot and killed eleven of them and wounded six others. The townsfolk of Ierapetra remained inside their homes for the five hours the guerrillas rampaged through the town but three children who had ventured out of doors to watch what was happening were hit by stray bullets. The gendarmes repelled attacks on their post but one gendarme was killed and six wounded, three seriously. Eventually the guerrillas began to withdraw, taking their three dead and two wounded men with them.

The two trucks, laden with booty, were driven eight kilometres out of town to a spot where other guerrillas were waiting. Most of the food and blankets were transferred to mules, which were led off into the mountains. One of the wounded, an army deserter from Agios Nikolaos, was taken to Doctor Hourdakis in Malles. Hourdakis had worked with ELAS during the occupation but also had good relations with Bandouvas: for two years he had hidden Bandouvas' wife from the Germans, passing her off as an aunt from Neapolis.

The brief seizure of Ierapetra caused outrage among the island's leaders and a search for the guerrillas began in earnest. A mixed force of gendarmes and soldiers and a large armed following under Manoli Bandouvas combined to comb the Dikti Mountains. Eventually, late one afternoon, they came across Podias and his men hiding near Kroustas. The guerrillas attempted to escape but found themselves virtually surrounded and forced to give battle. After four hours the guerrillas managed to slip away into the mountains as it grew dark, leaving behind them one dead guerrilla and some blankets and food that had been taken from Ierapetra.

Deciding that his best course was to return to his former base, Podias ordered Roukounakis and half a dozen men to maintain a presence near Kroustas and seek more recruits from the area while he led the rest of his men south, towards Kalamafka. Podias and his band were pursued for the rest of the night. There was occasional contact between the two sides and by morning seven guerrillas had been captured. These men were sent under strong guard to Heraklion along with two gendarmes who had been wounded in the fighting. To facilitate their getaway, Podias divided his band into two with instructions to rendezvous at Kalamafka two days later.

One of the armed bands escaped unhindered but the other was discovered, surrounded and attacked. In a bloody engagement, five guerrillas and one soldier were killed and five gendarmes wounded. The guerrilla survivors split into small groups and managed to make their way safely to the rendezvous point. Despite unrelenting patrols, no further trace could be found of Podias' men. Spotter planes that patrolled over the mountains during the day on the lookout for the guerrillas reported no sign of movement.

A couple of days later, Bandouvas and his men came across a single guerrilla who was guarding a cave high above Kalamafka. They killed the guerrilla and inside the cave discovered much of the foodstuff that had been stolen from Ierapetra and a large quantity of ammunition. Later that afternoon, Bandouvas' men killed two more guerrillas and captured five others. On the same day an army patrol discovered and arrested the wounded guerrilla who had been left in the care of Doctor Hourdakis at Malles.

Little food was given to the guerrillas voluntarily and with the loss of their provisions stored in the cave they were compelled to raid villages to survive. But the aggressive gendarme and army patrols made life difficult for them. One night a few armed men appeared in Prina demanding food but before they had finished collecting supplies were forced to flee when a lookout reported the approach of an army patrol. Another body of guerrillas arrived in the small village of Gergeri late one evening, gathered the villagers into the square and demanded food. A reported sighting of an approaching gendarme patrol interrupted the guerrillas in their work and they fled. A week later 30 armed men entered the village of Agios Vassilios and forcibly took food from the inhabitants. Within hours of their departure a large gendarme force was on their trail.

The party led by Roukounakis was the first to be liquidated. A few days after splitting from Podias' main band, he and his men were ambushed by an army patrol near Kroustas. Two of the men, both army deserters from Agios Nikolaos, were wounded and taken prisoner. Roukounakis escaped with four guerrillas but a few days later they were ambushed again and Roukounakis, wounded in the engagement, was the only one to escape with his life.

With search parties hunting for them in the Kalamafka area, Podias and his men began to make their way westward. En route, a band of fifty attacked the gendarme post at Kassanos one night. Four of the eight gendarmes defending the post were killed and the other four taken hostage. When news of the attack became known, a gendarme patrol and a large band of men under Christos Bandouvas set off in pursuit to rescue the prisoners. Three of the hostages were soon released but the body of the fourth gendarme was found the following day by Bandouvas' men.

Following the attack on Kassanos, Manoli Bandouvas announced a reward of ten million drachmas for information leading to the capture, dead or alive, of Yanni Podias, Mitsos Paparaftis and Yanni Roukounakis. He also gave assurances that if a guerrilla provided the information that led to the capture of one of the three men he would be given an amnesty and helped to relocate to another part of the country.

The announcement of the rewards was followed up with the arrests in Lasithi of those believed to have helped the guerrillas by supplying them with food and information. Seventeen men were detained in Ierapetra, eight in Sitia, four in Agios Nikolaos and a handful of others in the smaller villages. Within a week the first court martial was held in Heraklion. The wounded deserter who had been captured at Malles was sentenced to death. Three of the others on trial were sentenced to twenty years' imprisonment and another ten received fifteen-year sentences.

The search for Podias, roaming the southern Dikti Mountains with 85 men, was intensified. Early one morning in early June an army patrol discovered his hiding-place and launched an attack as soon as reinforcements reached them. Podias' men were well armed with mortars and heavy machine guns and fought off the attackers for the whole day. In the evening the guerrillas split up and made use of the cover provided by the forest to escape deeper into the mountains. Six guerrillas and two soldiers were killed in the engagement and ten soldiers wounded.

A few days later, Podias' men regrouped between Megali Vrissi and Larani, Podias' native village. Their pursuers were not far behind. The guerrillas were surrounded again late in the afternoon and forced to give battle. As before, they defended themselves until it grew dark and then fled through the woods. One guerrilla was killed and two badly wounded guerrillas were captured. All of Podias' relatives in Larani were arrested the day after the battle.

Podias split his followers into smaller groups and told them to head west for Mount Ida. One band led by Vassili Plagiotakis, a native of Embaros, was ordered to remain in the Dikti Mountains and organise a recruiting campaign when things had quietened down.

But Plagiotakis did not get the opportunity to carry out his mission. Near Embaros early on the morning of 27 June, he and twelve of his men were ambushed and killed; the three survivors, all army deserters, were captured. Bandouvas and the gendarmes took the dead bodies and their prisoners to Heraklion in triumph and declared Lasithi prefecture to be under complete government control.

Podias' men came together again on the south-eastern slopes of Mount Ida. They were joined by George Sbokos and his men and another group of armed men from Melambes. All the guerrillas remaining in eastern Crete, numbering around 80, had finally assembled in one place. Hunting for them was a large force of soldiers and gendarmes and Manoli Bandouvas with his private army of almost 200 men. Spotter planes once more flew over the mountains in an effort to pinpoint the guerrillas' exact position.

At 5 am on 28 June, the guerrillas ambushed a small patrol of gendarmes near Nidha plateau. Unknown to the guerrillas, there was a larger patrol of gendarmes nearby who immediately ran to the assistance of their comrades when they heard shots being fired. After four hours the guerrillas were forced to flee. The gendarmes lost three men killed and four wounded, but jubilation broke out when the body of Mitsos Paparaftis, Podias' second-in-command, was found on the battlefield.

The Eagles of Crete

The guerrillas split up once more and made their way southwest towards Melambes. Many of the guerrillas had no food and little water, and they were in a part of the mountains where there were few springs. Government forces were in hot pursuit and on several occasions skirmished with the bands of exhausted guerrillas. Twelve of the men were eventually surrounded near Agia Paraskevi and attacked by an army patrol. Four of the guerrillas were killed and three surrendered.

The band with Podias scattered and took cover among some tall oak trees near Lohria but was spotted by a large search party of gendarmes and soldiers. Podias and nine of the men with him were surrounded and, one by one, were shot and killed.

Podias' body was taken to Agia Varvara, where the nationalists, soldiers and gendarmes who had been pursuing him assembled. A convoy of cars and trucks was arranged and Podias' head and right hand were cut off and stuck on the end of long poles. The head was put on display in the lead jeep; Podias' hand was placed on display in the second vehicle; in another truck were four guerrilla prisoners.

It was late afternoon when the convoy arrived in Heraklion. Word that Podias had been killed spread quickly and a crowd soon gathered. Church bells rang out as the cars drove up to the government offices. From the balcony, several of the town's leading citizens made speeches welcoming the victory over Podias' band. Podias' head was then sent to the town's suburbs to be paraded around as proof that he was dead.

The following day, Bandouvas toured the villages making speeches and appealing to the villagers to hand over their weapons. Fifty rifles were surrendered. On the same day, the wounded Roukounakis emerged from his hiding-place and turned himself in to the nearest gendarme post. There were a few guerrillas on the run near Melambes but the authorities were confident that these men would soon surrender. Eastern Crete was declared free of insurgents.

The hunt for these remaining guerrillas died down and the survivors were able to make contact with each other. After a discussion, a handful, including George Sbokos, chose to remain in hiding in eastern

Crete but the rest decided to make their way to the west and join up with the larger guerrilla force that was active in Canea prefecture.

The men set off on the long journey through unfamiliar territory towards the White Mountains. On the way two of them were killed in a skirmish with some gendarmes, alerting the authorities to their movement. Eventually, after several nights' walk, the survivors of Podias' band, including nine of the deserters from the army camp at Agios Nikolaos, linked up with their comrades in the west at Kallikratis. They arrived in a sorry state: several had wrapped rags around their feet to replace their worn-out boots and all were bedraggled and starving.

The rebellion in eastern Crete had lasted just forty-five days from beginning to end.

Chapter 5
Unrest in the West

Just after midday on 24 May 1947, fifty guerrillas led by *Kapetan* George stopped the bus near Floria as it made its way to Kandanos. The passengers were ordered off and the guerrillas took their places. All weapons were kept out of sight as the driver obeyed his instructions to continue his journey and to park very close to the gendarme post in Kandanos.

On arrival, a handful of guerrillas stayed with the bus and driver while the remainder split into two groups. One group approached the gendarme post on foot and ordered the sentry to surrender. The young guard, startled by the sudden appearance of the armed guerrillas, panicked and opened fire. He was immediately shot and killed but the gunshots alerted the six other gendarmes of the garrison, who fired on the guerrillas. A brief battle took place in which two more gendarmes were killed; the remaining four surrendered. The post was ransacked and all food, clothing and weapons were taken. In the meantime, the second group of guerrillas burst into the post office and demanded that the manager open the safe. When he refused they shot and wounded him and ran off empty-handed.

With their booty and four gendarme hostages, the guerrillas got back onto the bus and set off towards Floria. After a while, they abandoned the bus and made off with their hostages on foot for Palea Roumata. Along the way, the captive gendarmes were set free, having first been dispossessed of their boots and uniforms.

Gyparis set out for Palea Roumata as soon as he was informed that *Kapetan* George and his men were heading that way. When word that Gyparis was approaching reached Palea Roumata, the villagers fled to the mountains. Gyparis arrived in Palea Roumata to find the village almost deserted.

The next morning, Gyparis went to Kandanos and found the inhabitants incensed at the guerrilla raid and demanding that firm action be taken. Gyparis made a speech to the assembled crowd and gave his word that the guerrillas would pay for their attack.

While speaking, Gyparis received information that twenty of the guerrillas who had taken part in the attack on Kandanos, were in Kakodiki, where some of them lived. He immediately ordered his men back into their trucks and drove to engage them. Meanwhile, the leader of this guerrilla party, Eftichis Litsardakis, had heard that Gyparis was in the area and decided to make for the safety of the mountains with his men. They had only just left Kakodiki when Gyparis arrived in the village. Gyparis set off in pursuit.

It was not long before the guerrillas were spotted on the bare mountainside as they approached a ridge. Gyparis' men hurriedly fired off mortar rounds, one of which landed right in the middle of the band. Taking what cover they could find the guerrillas opened fire on their pursuers. As two officers led a platoon to cut off the guerrillas, the rest of Gyparis' men kept them pinned down by heavy machine-gun fire.

The firing continued for some time but eventually ten of the guerrillas, five of whom were wounded, surrendered. Eight of the band had been killed, including Litsardakis. Only two guerrillas escaped and one of these was arrested a few days later at Souda while attempting to board a boat for Piraeus.

Two of Gyparis' men received slight wounds in the engagement and were sent back by truck to Canea. The weapons the guerrillas were armed with - German and Italian rifles and British Tommy guns - were gathered up and Gyparis proceeded to Kakodiki. Inside Litsardakis' home several gendarme uniforms, some dynamite and hand grenades were discovered.

On the last day of May, a band of 40 guerrillas under *Kapetan* George Spanoudakis set out from Ramni as soon as it grew dark and reached a hide-out near Embrosneros before dawn. During the morning an unarmed guerrilla was sent into Georgioupolis to obtain information on the gendarmes' movements and to reconnoitre the area. He was to rejoin his comrades at a farmhouse just outside Georgioupolis that night.

When dusk fell the guerrillas moved to the farmhouse. Their spy arrived later with his report that the gendarmes had been out on patrol that morning but had since returned to Georgioupolis, where they were billeted in the station itself and a nearby house. The garrison was believed to number ten men.

As they drew near to Georgioupolis, a few men took up positions on the Rethymnon/Canea road to prevent the arrival of reinforcements. Spanoudakis led the rest into the village. The guerrillas moved forward cautiously but suddenly firing broke out on all sides and the guerrillas realised they had walked into a trap. They returned fire, and in the confusion Spanoudakis fell to the ground, wounded in his side. It was later learned that he had been shot by one of his own men as he ran forward in the darkness. His wound was bandaged and four of his men were detailed to carry him to safety.

As the guerrillas began to withdraw one of them was killed, and just outside Georgioupolis a group of armed men was spotted coming from the direction in which the guerrillas planned to retreat. The guerrillas fired mortar shells at the armed band, scattering them temporarily.

It soon became clear that it was impossible to carry Spanoudakis for any great distance and he was hidden nearby. Two men stayed to look after him and another guerrilla hurried to Alikambos to fetch a doctor to tend to his wound. The main body of guerrillas pushed on to Ramni, arriving in the village just before dawn.

Spanoudakis was seen by a doctor and remained hidden for two days. He had lost a lot of blood but on the evening of the second day, as soon as it grew dark, the two men looking after him put him on a mule and set out for Ramni. They were met by a group of guerrillas who were returning to escort their leader to safety. Spanoudakis greeted them and seemed to be in good spirits but, a few hours later, on the outskirts of Fres, he died.

News of his death spread rapidly. Spanoudakis had served as an ELAS *kapetan* during the occupation and people from nearby villages arrived to pay their respects to a man that many regarded as a hero of the resistance. Spanoudakis' body was taken to the church in Ramni and the local priest conducted the funeral service. A dozen guerrillas fired a volley over his grave.

In the middle of June a new wave of unrest broke out in Kissamos. Roadblocks were put up at several points and a large band of guerrillas was reported to be gathering in Sassalos in preparation for a major attack. On 19 June, Gyparis was near Kandanos, touring the villages and making public speeches to the assembled villagers. When he heard of the large number of armed men at Sassalos he decided to move against them.

Usually, Gyparis sat in the front passenger seat of the lead vehicle when on patrol but on the drive to Sassalos that day he decided to switch places with Manousos Karkanis, a former EOK leader from Imbros, and seated himself in the second vehicle in the convoy.

As Gyparis' column approached Floria it was fired upon by guerrillas hiding on the hillside. Karkanis was hit in the head by the first burst of gunfire. The gendarmes jumped from their trucks and returned fire and in a short time the guerrillas retreated. The body of one dead guerrilla was found and large traces of blood at the scene suggested that at least one other guerrilla had been seriously wounded.

Karkanis died shortly after the shooting stopped. His body was taken back to his village and buried the following day. A huge crowd turned out to follow his coffin and pay respects to the venerable resistance leader. After the funeral, many of Karkanis' male relatives and close friends took their weapons and set off for Kissamos to seek revenge.

On the day of Karkanis' funeral, a large band of armed men led by *Kapetan* George held up the morning bus as it set out for Canea from Vathi. All the passengers except Stefanos Kamilakis, a staunch nationalist, were told to get off the bus. The driver was ordered to drive to Koutsamatados, where the guerrillas abandoned the vehicle and set off with their hostage on the donkey path to Sassalos.

When Kiriakos Kamilakis heard that his uncle had been kidnapped by the guerrillas he called together his relatives and friends and began to round up leftists in Kastelli. The authorities swiftly intervened and pleaded with him to release his hostages. Kamilakis eventually agreed to do so provided that four of the men he released would go to Sassalos, find the guerrillas and persuade them to free his uncle.

That night the guerrillas seized four more hostages from Topolia and Potamida. The four leftists released by Kamilakis caught up with the guerrillas the following day and persuaded them to free their most recent hostages. However, the guerrilla leaders were adamant they would not release Stefanos Kamilakis, the uncle, and executed him later that day.

Uproar broke out when the news of Stefanos Kamilakis' murder reached Kastelli. Many fled the small town for the neighbouring villages: the nationalists because they believed a rumour that the communists were on their way to Kastelli to attack the gendarme post and burn the town, and the leftists because they feared reprisals from the nationalists in Kastelli. Gyparis hastened to Kastelli to keep order.

Meanwhile, the relatives and friends of the murdered Stefanos Kamilakis had gathered in a house just outside Topolia. Soon after dusk they were warned that armed men were approaching the village. Assuming the men were guerrillas, the Kamilakis party took up positions on the path along which the armed men were coming and as soon as they came into sight opened fire on them. The armed men fired back and an intense gunfight broke out; it was several minutes before the Kamilakis family discovered that they were firing on members of the Karkanis family, who had come from Imbros to seek revenge on the guerrillas.

The battle ceased and both sides inspected their casualties. Nicholas Karkanis, a brother of the murdered Manousos, had been shot and killed and another brother, Artemis, had been wounded in the shoulder. On the Kamilakis side, Emmanuel Kamilakis, the eighteen-year-old son of the murdered Stefanos, had been seriously wounded. He was taken to hospital in Canea but died of his wounds.

Less than a month after the failed attack on the gendarme post at Georgioupolis, the guerrillas were once more gathering in force near

Palea Roumata. For several weeks there had been contact between the guerrilla leadership and two of the aircraftsmen at Maleme airfield, who wished to join the guerrillas. One of the aircraftsmen was a sergeant–major who protected his identity by adopting the pseudonym *Kapetan* Youras; the other was Stamatis Mariolis, a former member of EPON from Sparta in the Peloponnese. The two aircraftsmen agreed to surrender the base to the guerrillas one night when Mariolis was the guard on duty.

Kapetan Mihali and *Kapetan* George ordered their guerrillas to be ready for action on the night of 1 July and a rumour was deliberately spread that an attack was planned on the gendarme post at Voukolies, thus ensuring that the coming raid on the aerodrome could not be betrayed.

Early in the evening of 1 July, the guerrillas commandeered the Palea Roumata bus and a lorry that was used for taking charcoal to Canea. Using minor roads, the two vehicles set off crammed with guerrillas and arrived at the aerodrome at the pre-arranged time. The telephone wires to Canea and Kastelli were cut and a small number of guerrillas prepared an ambush to prevent the arrival of any government troops during the operation. As Mariolis swung open the gates the guerrillas silently entered the aerodrome.

When all the buildings were under their control, *Kapetan* Mihali walked into the dormitory with some of his men and announced to the sleepy conscripts that the Democratic Army had taken over the base. He ordered them to load up the aerodrome's three trucks and jeep with anything of value that could be moved.

All the weapons, including three heavy machine guns, were loaded into the trucks. Uniforms, blankets, food, and all the military equipment they could carry, including the base radio, were taken. The guerrillas and the 57 aircraftsmen at the base got on board the vehicles and the convoy set off on its roundabout route back to Palea Roumata.

On arrival in the village, everything was unloaded from the trucks and either concealed nearby or put onto mules and taken up into the mountains to be hidden in caves. All the tyres were removed to provide

The Eagles of Crete

soles for the guerrillas' boots. Soles made from tyres were heavy but durable and much quieter on the mountain tracks than hobnailed boots.

Gyparis heard the news of the raid on Maleme a few hours after it took place and immediately set off for Palea Roumata. When he arrived in the village he found it almost deserted, the inhabitants having fled on news of his approach. He sent out patrols into the surrounding hills but these returned after several hours with little to report. Only one patrol chanced upon any guerrillas. Caught off-guard, as they lay resting in an olive grove, two guerrillas were killed and a third was wounded and captured.

Meanwhile the conscript aircraftsmen had been taken to a hideout where various guerrilla leaders harangued them for two days in an attempt to persuade them to change sides. Only seven of the aircraftsmen chose to remain in the mountains and the rest made it clear that they wished to return to their base.

The guerrillas did not prevent the 50 aircraftsmen from leaving, but before they let them go they took their uniforms and boots. Having made their way to Alikianos, the aircraftsmen presented themselves at the gendarme post. They were immediately placed under arrest, treated as captured guerrillas and taken to the prison at Firka fortress in Canea. There they were kept for several weeks, awaiting deportation to the mainland.

While Gyparis was patrolling the area around Palea Roumata in a vain search for the perpetrators of the raid on Maleme, Manoli Pissadakis and Yanni Bandourakis joined forces and moved to the hills near Malaxa.

After hiding out during the day they set off as soon as darkness fell and descended to Chrisopigi, just three kilometres from Canea. Nearby was a large workshop that had been built by the Germans to repair all their vehicles in Crete. The workshop had been left intact by the Germans at the end of the occupation and it was well stocked with spare parts, all sorts of machinery and a large quantity of petrol. Most of the soldiers serving there were unarmed mechanics.

The telephone wires were cut and the soldiers were roused from their sleep. Trucks were loaded up with food, blankets and weapons as the guerrillas set about destroying the workshop itself.

Petrol was poured on wooden benches, tyres and two trucks the guerrillas were not taking with them. Flames leapt high into the air, lighting up the sky, and word quickly spread in Canea that there was an enormous fire at Chrisopigi.

The twenty-five soldiers and two officers at the workshop were forced into the trucks at gunpoint. As they drove up the zigzag road towards Malaxa, the blazing workshop was visible below. One of the trucks broke down near Gerolakkos but its load was quickly transferred and by sunrise the guerrillas were in Drakona.

An infantry company set off from Canea in hot pursuit of the guerrillas and soon came across the abandoned truck at Gerolakkos. On learning that the guerrillas were in Drakona the troops made straight for the village. Taken by surprise at the speed of the pursuit, the guerrillas took to the hills but were spotted by the soldiers as they climbed a donkey path. The troops opened fire with mortars and machine guns; a few guerrillas took cover and returned fire, allowing their comrades to carry out a successful retreat.

The abducted soldiers resisted all attempts to persuade them to throw in their lot with the guerrillas and join the Democratic Army. When it became clear to the guerrilla leaders that the soldiers were unmoved by their arguments they were allowed to return to Canea, after first being relieved of their uniforms and boots.

Outraged at the guerrilla successes in Crete, the Athens government ordered a battalion of 500 soldiers from Heraklion to reinforce Gyparis. Bandouvas offered to move to western Crete with his private army of 200 men but Gyparis assured him that the force at his disposal would be sufficient for the job of dealing with the threat from the guerrillas around Canea.

On 18 July, a large number of guerrillas under Bandourakis and Pissadakis blocked the road near Gerolakkos. One of the first trucks to come along was driven by 36-year-old Nikos Papadakis, who was on his way to Canea with a load of wood. During the occupation, Papadakis had been a local company commander for EOK. In recent months he had shown no open hostility to former members of EAM-ELAS, nor had he been openly critical of the strikes or spoken publicly against the left.

Many of the guerrillas respected Papadakis as a former nationalist resistance leader in the area, but they also recognised that he was a potential enemy. There had been a rumour for some time that Gyparis had offered Papadakis the opportunity to recruit armed men and help to wipe out the guerrillas. Papadakis had turned down the offer, hoping that the rebellion in Crete would soon blow over, but some of the guerrillas were afraid that he would not remain neutral forever. Papadakis' truck was brought to a halt at the guerrilla roadblock.

The decision was taken to kill Papadakis. Several guerrillas were opposed to the idea but found themselves in the minority and failed to persuade their comrades to release him. The guerrillas took Papadakis' watch, wedding ring and money, set fire to his truck and took him on a path up the hillside. Some way from the road, his executioners stabbed him in the chest and throat, gouged out an eye and then shot him in the back of the head. His body was left beside the path.

That evening, as news of Papadakis' abduction reached Canea, two brothers of Xenophon Kodinidis, a guerrilla, were seized by armed men who, unaware that Papadakis was already dead, announced that the brothers would be held until Papadakis was released. Later, friends of Papadakis took hostage two more men, one a relative of Pissadakis and the other a left-wing teacher. Stefanos Proimos, a former senior ELAS officer, and the lawyers Adam Aretakis, Stavros Hatzigrigoris and Adonis Kornarakis were also apprehended. Two retired, disabled army officers, 49-year-old Lt Colonel George Stamatakis and 51-year-old Colonel George Papoutsakis were also seized. All the hostages were taken to Souda and locked in a small house. During the night, Kornarakis managed to escape through a small window but instead of returning home he took to the mountains and joined the guerrillas.

Papadakis' body was found the following morning and news of his death quickly reached Souda. Stamatakis and Papoutsakis, who had both worked with EAM during the occupation, were taken outside by their captors and shot.

As soon as Gyparis heard of the deaths of the two retired army officers he intervened to secure the release of the remaining hostages. All of them returned to their homes except the lawyer, Stavros Hatzigrigoris, who sought safety in the mountains. He had previously been beaten up on the way to his office and after his abduction feared for his life in Canea. But Hatzigrigoris was to find life in the mountains particularly hard. Unlike most of the guerrillas he adapted poorly to night marches and sleeping rough; he also had the added problem of being short-sighted.

When news of the death of Papadakis reached Kastelli, 50 right-wingers rampaged through the town attacking the homes of left-wingers, burning down a shop and a dentist's surgery. Houses of known left-wingers in Potamida and Trialonia were set ablaze. That night a large number of rightists appeared outside the home of Manoli Bandourakis in Kourphalona. Up until then, 72-year-old Manoli, father of the guerrilla leader Yanni Bandourakis, had been left to live his life in peace. The nationalists seized the old man, took him to the outskirts of the village and shot him. They then set fire to his house and broke open all his barrels of olive oil, pouring the contents into the ground. The house owned by Zacharias Bandourakis, a cousin of the guerrilla leader, was also destroyed, his wife and two children taking refuge with neighbours.

Another large band of armed right-wingers collected in Kolimbari where they began terrorising their political opponents. When they heard that a group of right-wingers was burning houses in and around Kastelli they moved west to join up with them. In Kastelli there was panic at a rumour that *Kapetan* George was advancing from Elos with over 100 guerrillas, abducting nationalist hostages and burning houses in reprisal for the murder of Manoli Bandourakis. The following day, the local gendarme commander sent word to his superiors in Canea that public order had broken down and that he was unable to restrain the nationalists.

Gyparis ordered the army to Kissamos to restore order. *Kapetan* George, on learning that soldiers were arriving in force in Kastelli, promptly withdrew southwards. Two of the six hostages he had taken were executed near Sirikari; the four others were released the next day.

The army made straight for the guerrilla stronghold around Elos, forcing the guerrillas to retreat south towards Chrissoskalitissa. To the surprise of the guerrillas, the soldiers set up camp at Elos and began a systematic search of the area. In the past the army had carried out brief patrols before moving on but on this occasion it was clear that the soldiers intended to remain in the locality for some time. Over the following days the army patrols searched the area thoroughly without success: the guerrillas had split up and melted away.

While the army was busy around Elos, Gyparis planned an attack on around 40 guerrillas that were permanently based in the Ramni area. With his special force, the Gypari, he set off by truck at midnight for Agii Pandes. As the trucks drew near to the village the drivers switched off their headlights so that any lookouts placed by the guerrillas would be unable to determine the exact number of vehicles. From the village, Gyparis led his men on foot towards Ramni.

The guerrillas had spent the night sleeping outside the village and, just as it was getting light, were awoken by a villager with news that the Gypari were heading directly for them. After hurriedly filling their water bottles, the guerrillas made for the mountains.

Before they had gone far, Gyparis' men appeared on the hillside and opened fire. To avoid being surrounded, the guerrillas fired off a few shots and kept moving, hoping to outstrip their pursuers and reach safety. The steep, rocky terrain with its numerous gullies was in the guerrillas' favour but as more and more gendarmes arrived they found that retreat was impossible. They had little alternative but to take up a strong defensive position and attempt to hold out until they were able to slip away later in the day.

For eight hours the shooting between the two sides continued, with the guerrillas unable to escape and the gendarmes unable to advance. Eventually, in the heat of the afternoon, the guerrillas made their getaway, leaving five dead comrades behind them and abandoning two machine guns and several rifles. Two guerrillas were captured and two of Gyparis' men were slightly wounded in the engagement.

Gyparis now turned his attention westward. A gendarme and a soldier had recently been killed in a night attack near Agia and their killers were reported to have escaped in the direction of Nea Roumata. On the day before Gyparis planned to launch his attack, planes flew over the area dropping leaflets warning the villagers to stay in their homes and calling on the guerrillas to surrender.

Just after midnight, several trucks full of soldiers set off from Canea for Nea Roumata. Leaving the trucks in the village, the soldiers split into three platoons and made their way towards Prasses. Contact was soon made between one platoon and a large force of guerrillas, who put up a stout resistance for several hours. Mortar rounds were fired by both sides and the guerrillas eventually retreated towards the wooded slopes of Apopigadi. One soldier was killed and four wounded but it was not until later that morning that the soldiers came across the guerrilla casualties. In a clearing they found a guerrilla who had been seriously wounded and the bodies of three of his comrades.

Pursuit of the guerrillas continued and the following morning an army patrol surprised five guerrillas on Apopigadi. In the brief battle two of the guerrillas, both armed with machine guns, were killed. Army search parties patrolled Apopigadi for some time but the guerrillas avoided all further contact and gave their pursuers the slip.

On his return to Canea, Gyparis announced that his own private force would be increased by a hundred men. He also gave orders that all villagers in the prefecture of Canea should hand in their weapons forthwith to their nearest gendarme station, and he imposed a stricter curfew in the countryside.

A few days after this announcement, gendarmes ambushed a small group of guerrillas as they cut down the telephone wires near Voukolies. The guerrillas returned fire and retreated towards Palea Roumata without loss. The following day the workers who were repairing telephone wires outside Messavlia were held up by another party of guerrillas who stole their tools before fleeing eastwards. As these guerrillas were believed to be hiding in the Palea Roumata area,

The Eagles of Crete

Gyparis ordered the soldiers who were still based in Elos to march on Palea Roumata from the west. Gyparis set off with his men by truck to Nea Roumata and approached Palea Roumata on foot from the east.

On Gyparis' arrival in Palea Roumata, the villagers were summoned to the square and Gyparis made a brief speech demanding the surrender of all the weapons in the village. Over a hundred guns were reluctantly handed in and a house-to-house search uncovered even more firearms. A careful search of one house led to the discovery and arrest of the wife of *Kapetan* George. Originally from Asia Minor, Eudoxia Kalfa had been hiding for some time in Palea Roumata with her two children, aged three and eighteen months.

Yanni Bandourakis was on the Omalos plateau when he learnt of the murder of his father. To his men he showed little emotion, shrugging it off as a misfortune that was an expected part of the struggle. Most of his men were suffering from stomach problems that they attributed to the cheese they had had been eating and many of them were despondent at the news of all the reverses the guerrillas had suffered recently.

The arrival of his eldest son, Manoli, escorted to Omalos by a comrade from his village, cheered Bandourakis immensely. Bandourakis had five children but following the death of his father was particularly concerned that his eldest son would be the next target of assassination for the nationalists.

Bandourakis remained on the Omalos plateau, occasionally meeting with the other *kapetans* and discussing plans for action. There were constant alarms that an army raid on their base was imminent.

In late August a messenger arrived at the guerrilla camp with information that there was a large amount of food stored in the monastery of Agia Triada at Perivolia. For the guerrillas this seemed too good an opportunity to miss. Perivolia was dangerously close to Canea but Bandourakis calculated that he would be able to make a surprise raid on the monastery and return to the safety of the mountains before the alarm could be given. At midday he left on the long walk to Therisso with 30 men.

At mid-morning the following day Bandourakis and his men collected some mules from the village and started out on the three-hour trek to the monastery. They approached the monastery unobserved and took the abbot and his monks by surprise as they burst in through the gates. The abbot was held at gunpoint while the monks carried out the guerrillas' orders and opened up their warehouse. For the next hour the guerrillas loaded up the mules with vast quantities of grain and olive oil. As soon as they had finished they hastened back to Therisso.

The following day was spent hiding the food in safe places between Therisso and Drakona. Around midday the first army patrol arrived to search the area and chanced upon a few guerrillas. A brief gun battle ensued. One soldier was slightly wounded in the leg and the guerrillas, realising they were outnumbered and that there might be other patrols in the area, retreated into the hills. For the rest of the day, army patrols scoured the area without any success.

That night the guerrillas gathered together under the ancient plane trees at Aliakes spring, south of Therisso. For the whole of the following day they remained in hiding but during the night moved down the mountain to Meskla. They arrived in the village soon after dawn, roused the bus driver from his bed and ordered him to take them to Fournes.

On their arrival in Fournes, several villagers were on the streets and a few had already gone to work in the fields. The guerrillas cut the telephone line and went round the houses ordering the inhabitants to assemble in the square. As soon as a sizeable crowd had gathered, Bandourakis addressed his audience at great length, assuring his listeners that the Democratic Army would win the civil war and appealing to them for their help and support. At the end of his speech, the guerrillas sang ELAS resistance songs to the villagers before getting back on board the bus and returning to Meskla. As a precaution, they took the village telephone with them.

It was mid-morning when the guerrillas arrived in Meskla and they immediately set off back into the mountains. Later that day, while the guerrillas were resting, a shepherd came to Bandourakis with a rumour that there was a considerable amount of clothing and footwear in the village of Karanos that was part of a consignment of aid from the United Nations Relief and Rehabilitation Association (UNRRA), which had been sent to Crete for distribution among the poor and needy. According to the rumour, the village president had refused to distribute the aid among the villagers and was keeping it under lock and key for his family's use. Most of the UNRRA aid which had earlier arrived in Crete had been gratefully received and distributed: hundreds of mules from the USA and Brazil had been landed by US steamer at the beginning of the year and had already been put to work by their new owners. Four hundred Australian horses that had arrived in Heraklion were considered unsuitable for the terrain and had been sent to Kavala, but clothing and, in particular, footwear were in short supply on Crete and were never refused. Bandourakis made plans to pay a visit to Karanos the following night.

To avoid detection, the guerrillas took a long, roundabout route on minor tracks to Karanos and remained in hiding until it began to get dark. When the lookouts reported that it was safe to do so, Bandourakis led his men into the village. The president expressed astonishment when Bandourakis demanded the UNRRA footwear and clothing be handed over and explained that all the aid that had arrived in the village had been distributed months earlier. After a careful search, Bandourakis was forced to accept that what the village president said was true.

For the guerrillas the long walk to Karanos had ended in disappointment and they now had to face the long climb to Omalos, where Bandourakis had planned to spend the night. After two hours they reached the col at Fokies and the guerrillas debated whether to continue their march to the plateau that night or whether to sleep on a hill near the mule path and continue the trek first thing in the morning. The majority, including Bandourakis, were in favour of spending the night where they were so they made for the hill of Boubounokefala, just to the east of Fokies, and settled down for the night.

Since Bandourakis' raid on the monastery several army patrols had been searching the mountains for the guerrillas. By chance, an infantry company was making for Fokies on the same night that Bandourakis and his men were preparing to bivouac on Boubounokefala. The company commander had decided to spend the night in the vicinity of Fokies and as they approached the col one of the soldiers in the vanguard heard voices and he became suspicious that a number of guerrillas were nearby.

Two soldiers moved stealthily forward until they were able to establish beyond doubt that guerrillas were occupying Boubounokefala. They returned to their commanding officer who decided it was too late at night to attack an unknown number of men. Orders were given to move forward as silently as possible and await the dawn.

As the sun came up the following morning some of Bandourakis' men were clearly discernible against the skyline as they rolled up their blankets and prepared to continue their march to Omalos. No guards had been set that night and the guerrillas were completely unaware that all their movements were being observed.

As the guerrillas began to move off, the soldiers opened fire. Two or three of the guerrillas were hit and fell; the rest rushed for cover. A gunfight broke out and continued for two hours, at the end of which two soldiers had been killed and four wounded. Several of the guerrillas escaped but three were captured. When the soldiers inspected the battlefield they counted thirteen enemy dead. Among them was Yanni Bandourakis.

The jubilant soldiers took Bandourakis' body down to the road at Lakki. There, they strung up his corpse on a scaffold in the back of a lorry and set off for Canea. At every village they stopped to display the former guerrilla leader's body to the inhabitants and when they reached Canea they drove the body around the streets of the town.

Hopes were high that with the death of Bandourakis the civil strife in Crete would soon be over.

Chapter 6
The Evacuation of the Villages

Three weeks after Bandourakis' death, the guerrilla leaders came together for a meeting in Zourva, which was also attended by the Secretary of the KKE in Crete, George Tsitilos, who had recently taken to the mountains. The guerrilla leader Manousakas had never been popular with the rank and file, and with the losses suffered recently there was an increasing belief that he was incapable of leading them to victory. At the meeting it was decided that *Kapetan* Mihali would replace Manousakas as military leader with Nikos Tsamantis as second-in-command.

A change of strategy was also agreed upon. Henceforth, the guerrillas would base themselves on the Omalos plateau, 1,100 metres above sea level. They were to steer clear of battles to avoid suffering casualties and if attacked on Omalos would retreat into the higher mountains or the wilderness of the Samaria Gorge. The Omalos plateau was far too big for the government forces to surround – it took one hour to cross it on foot - and there were paths out of it in all directions.

In contrast to the inactivity of the guerrillas, government forces increased the number of patrols and search parties and made many arrests in the villages that had given support to the guerrillas. Only one guerrilla lost his life during this period, in an ambush near Kares. The corpse was identified as that of Dimitri Rozakis and as proof that Rozakis had been killed the soldiers cut off his head and took it to Canea, where it was put on public display on the bridge over the Kladissos.

The death of Bandourakis had coincided with a change of government in Athens. Themistocles Sophoulis, the new prime minister, in an attempt to reduce the guerrilla force, offered an amnesty to the guerrillas and all those who had been assisting them in Crete. The amnesty was for crimes committed from the end of the German occupation up until 1 August 1947. All guerrillas who wished to take advantage of the amnesty were ordered to present themselves to the nearest army or gendarme post with their weapons. Those who had not taken part in the armed struggle but had supplied information, food and shelter to the guerrillas were promised they would suffer no persecution provided they confessed their past crimes. The amnesty applied to all Greeks on the island, not just the Cretans, as well as those who had failed to report for national service. This offer of amnesty was to be valid for a month.

Leaflets giving details of the amnesty were dropped from planes over the mountains and hill villages. As a gesture of good will, several wives and relatives of the guerrillas, many of them elderly, who had been charged with aiding the rebels, were released from prison.

Very soon there was a steady flow of guerrillas presenting themselves to military posts to surrender. One of the first to take advantage of the amnesty was Yanni Bandourakis' seventeen-year-old son, Manoli.

One of the senior, most experienced guerrillas who surrendered was Emmanuel Bikakis, who had been with Bandourakis from the beginning. The 29-year-old, from Kefalas in Kissamos, had recently commanded a small group of guerrillas that set up roadblocks near Kakopetros and the reward for his capture had been increased to twenty million drachmas. For several days after the announcement of the amnesty it was rumoured that he had been in contact with the Bishop of Kissamos and was about to surrender. The days went by and, just as the authorities decided that he had had a change of mind, he turned up one morning at the Gonia monastery at Kolimbari. The monks arranged for the local gendarmerie to collect him. Later in the day Bikakis was released and an announcement was made that the reward would not be paid out as Bikakis had surrendered voluntarily and had not been captured.

Several army deserters from the Canea area also took the opportunity provided by the amnesty to surrender. Villagers who came forward and admitted that they had helped the guerrillas in some way were released after they had signed a declaration of repentance and given their word to be law-abiding citizens in the future. The amnesty proved to be so successful that it was extended for another month.

For the communists, there was an urgent need to replace their comrades who were surrendering and after a meeting of the leadership it was agreed that Doctor Siganos would return to his native village in Heraklion prefecture and attempt to regenerate the Democratic Army in the eastern part of the island.

Manoli Siganos had been born in Skalani, near Heraklion, and had joined the KKE at an early age. He was serving time in Acronauplia prison when the Germans invaded Greece and was later transferred to the north of the country. As he was a doctor, he was sent to work in a sanatorium near Mount Olympus and was permitted to visit the sick in nearby villages. Given a great amount of freedom, he lost no time in making contact with EAM and when the opportunity presented itself he gave his escort the slip and joined up with the resistance.

Siganos was to take six guerrillas with him, all of whom were from eastern Crete and had served with Podias. One night they seized a boat at Loutro and sailed to Tsoutsouros Bay. On arrival they scattered, each to his own village, with orders to recruit supporters and carry out as much destruction and sabotage as they could.

However, one of the guerrillas had a change of heart after leaving his comrades and went to the gendarme post at Viannos where he surrendered with his weapon and asked for amnesty. Later that same day another guerrilla gave himself up to the gendarmes in Embaros. Alerted to the arrival of the rebels from the west, the gendarmes quickly rounded up the remaining four guerrillas. Dr Siganos alone slipped through the net and, at the end of October, managed to reach Melambes, where he went to ground with a family of communist sympathisers. His comrades spread a rumour that he had died of illness and after a time the authorities ceased looking for him.

Things were going from bad to worse for the guerrillas. Morale was low and, with the size of the Democratic Army decreasing daily, the

KKE leadership appealed to all its members to take to the mountains and join the fight for victory. The appeal was successful. However, many of these new recruits were young and inexperienced and some had not fired a gun before.

Among those who heeded the call and took to the mountains was Nikos Kokovlis, who had been in hiding in Canea for seven months. Remaining at liberty in town was becoming more and more difficult as the leftists were gradually being rounded up.

Kokovlis made for Vamvakopoulo and for several days hid near his family home, among the overgrown brambles and reeds by the banks of the Kladissos. His younger brother, Yakovos, provided him with food and news each day until a young guide collected him and took him to a hide-out near Varipetro. After a few days in hiding near the village, a dozen guerrillas arrived one night and took Kokovlis to Omalos.

On the Omalos Plateau Kokovlis was reunited with his sister, Pagona, an EPON activist who had recently taken to the mountains. There were seventeen female guerrillas under the command of Georgia Skevaki, from Trialonia, billeted in General Mandakas' old house, which was situated near the middle of the plateau. Most of the young women who had fled their homes had done so to be with their brothers who had joined the guerrillas. Many of them knew little about communism but they were fearful that as relatives of guerrillas they were liable to be arrested by the authorities. It was a difficult choice for the young women to make: to remain at home and face possible arrest and deportation or flee to the mountains and live with a rebel force of desperate, armed men. By choosing life in the mountains they lost the respect of the members of the communities they left behind.

One of the biggest problems faced by the Democratic Army was that of obtaining a regular supply of food and they often went hungry. There was rarely a shortage of olive oil but the guerrillas frequently went without bread, perhaps for a month or more at a time. One foodstuff they were not short of was potatoes: they appropriated the Omalos potato crop that belonged to farmers from Lakki, who no longer came to the plateau, and their meals often consisted solely of potatoes, fried or boiled on alternate days.

The Eagles of Crete

The authorities took advantage of the concentration of guerrilla forces on Omalos and made occasional air attacks on their positions. To guard against these surprise raids, the guerrillas placed a lookout on Kallergi hill with instructions to fire two shots as a warning of approaching planes. The main targets for the planes were the farm buildings on the plateau. When the warning shots were fired, the guerrillas would scuttle out of the huts and take shelter among nearby rocks. The planes would machine-gun and bomb the plateau but never succeeded in wounding a guerrilla. The worst damage that was ever done was to the guerrillas' lunch that was being prepared outside one of the huts. It was completely destroyed one day when a bomb scored a direct hit.

To improve their food supply and to obtain funds, the guerrillas were eventually forced to go on the offensive. Early one morning, twenty guerrillas descended on a shepherd as he watched over his flock of sheep outside Lakki. The shepherd was badly beaten and the sheep were driven off to Omalos. A few days later, 200 sheep were stolen by guerrillas from another hillside above Lakki.

Another ten men descended on the small village of Amigdalokefali in Kissamos after learning that the village president was collecting money to rebuild a house that had earlier been burnt down by the guerrillas. When it grew dark the guerrillas forced their way into the president's home and took over 500,000 drachmas.

At the highest point in the road between Messavlia and Floria seven armed men under *Kapetan* George patiently lay in wait for the bus as it made its way from Canea to Kandanos. When the bus came into view the guerrillas stood in the road and signalled the driver to stop. The driver attempted to drive through the ambush but the bus was brought to a halt when the guerrillas opened fire, wounding one of the female passengers in the leg. Passengers and driver were ordered from the bus and searched. A total of 920,000 drachmas was seized from them.

Among the passengers were two brothers from Sarakina. Besides these two, there were three other brothers in the family, one of whom was with the guerrillas in the mountains. One of the brothers on the bus that day, Mihali, was a gendarme who had been serving in the

Peloponnese and was on leave in Crete. When the guerrillas learnt that one of the passengers was a gendarme they began to beat him up, despite pleas from his brother and the other passengers. The off-duty gendarme was badly injured and, before fleeing the scene, one of the guerrillas shot him in the chest. The 24-year-old gendarme died in his brother's arms.

Not surprisingly, support for the communists in Crete, which had never been high, began to decline following this spate of savage attacks. More and more villagers began to turn against the guerrillas and inform the authorities of their movements, making it difficult for them to travel freely around the countryside.

One of those who had escaped from the Bandourakis ambush was Stelios Yakoumakis, who had spent a whole month hidden in his fiancée's house in Lakki and was making a good recovery from his shoulder wound. Word of his presence must have reached the authorities because early in the morning of 3 October the house in which he was hiding was searched by an army patrol. Yakoumakis was discovered and arrested. The officer in charge of the search party telephoned Canea and requested a truck and escort to take Yakoumakis to prison. Lt Foundoulakis, with three soldiers and two gendarmes, set off immediately from town to collect the prisoner.

By chance, a small body of guerrillas was preparing to ambush traffic that same morning on the road between Fournes and Lakki. This stretch of lonely, winding, mountain road provided the guerrillas with several suitable sites for an ambush.

When the army truck carrying Lt Foundoulakis and his men was spotted by the guerrillas they took cover and waited for it to reach their position. As it came level with them they opened up with machine-gun and rifle fire and one of the guerrillas tossed a grenade into the back of the truck. In the sudden hail of bullets, the driver and one of the gendarmes were killed instantly and the rest were wounded and unable to put up any resistance. The guerrillas spared the lives of the wounded men but took possession of all their weapons, boots and valuables before setting off for the mountains to the south. Despite their injuries, the five wounded men crawled for the shelter of nearby bushes, terrified that the guerrillas might return and execute them.

Later that day, the army officer in charge of the search party in Lakki rang Canea to find out why the escort had not arrived to collect his prisoner. When it was confirmed that the truck had set out from Canea several hours earlier, an army patrol was despatched down the road to look for it. The patrol moved warily but eventually came across the deserted truck and found the wounded men hiding in the bushes. The injured men were taken to Canea and Gyparis was informed of the ambush.

News of the ambush enraged the soldiers and villagers in Lakki. Yakoumakis was held responsible for the deaths of the two members of the escort and later that evening was taken to the square and shot.

For two days a company of Gyparis' men scoured the area south of the ambush spot without success. Just as they were about to give up the search, they came across seven guerrillas at Aliakes spring. It was early in the morning and the guerrillas, led by Pissadakis, were taken completely by surprise.

As they attempted to flee, Pissadakis was shot in the leg and was forced to take cover behind a boulder. His men immediately went to his assistance and attempted to carry him to safety. One of the Gypari was killed as the battle raged but the guerrillas realised they were in danger of being surrounded. In a final effort to save their leader, one of Pissadakis' men helped him to his feet but as he did so he was shot and killed. When the remaining guerrillas saw their comrade fall to the ground they abandoned their leader and made their escape.

By the time Gyparis' men inspected the battlefield Pissadakis had died of his wounds. In an act calculated to strike terror into the hearts of the guerrillas, Pissadakis' head and right hand were cut off and taken to Canea and put on public display. His family was allowed to collect the rest of the corpse and take it for burial.

A communist veteran, Pissadakis had taken a leading role in the foundation of the earliest resistance movement in the occupation and was one of the first to take to the mountains on the outbreak of civil war and his service to his country during the occupation was widely recognised by friend and foe alike. His death was a great loss to the guerrillas, especially as it came so soon after the death of Bandourakis.

Units for Defending the Countryside (MAY) had been established to protect villages in northern Greece the previous year and similar units were set up in villages in western Crete in the late summer of 1947. Loyal nationalists in each village were provided with weapons and warned to be ready for operations at short notice and to turn out to defend their village if attacked by guerrillas. The commanders selected to lead the new units were usually officers in the reserve who lived locally. All members of the MAY took an oath of loyalty to the government. However, the introduction of this new force did not stop the guerrillas targeting individual nationalists in their villages.

On the night of 18 October, around 30 guerrillas under *Kapetan* George left their base on Omalos and descended on Prines. By 5 am they had surrounded the village. As a small number of men broke into the home of Stamatis Sartzetakis, the rest opened fire on the home of one of his relatives. Fifty-two-year-old Stamatis was killed and his nineteen-year-old son was wounded. The guerrillas then set fire to the house, throwing into the flames the daughter's dowry that had been collected for her forthcoming wedding. A second house was set alight and the guerrillas, under fire from the villagers, retreated to Omalos, taking four hostages with them. Two of the hostages, a mother and her fourteen-year-old son, were released that evening, but the two other hostages, both teenage males, were executed.

The next attack took place in Palea Roumata, the former guerrilla stronghold, where the village president, Theodore Kouris, had learnt to live with threats against his life. One of the few nationalists in the village, he had stuck to his political convictions and, powerless to do otherwise, had turned a blind eye when armed men sought refuge in Palea Roumata. He had never informed on his neighbours but he was still considered an enemy and a potential threat by the guerrillas.

Just after 10 pm on 22 October, a dozen guerrillas dressed in gendarme uniforms knocked on the door of Kouris' home. On opening the door Kouris was seized and taken to the village school where he was questioned about his contacts with the gendarmerie for over an hour. At the end of his interrogation he was taken out into the schoolyard and shot in the head. A few days later the guerrillas returned to the village and burnt down the house of the village priest.

A week later, at 2 o'clock in the morning, Nikos Tsamantis and twenty guerrillas arrived at the home of Constantine Kaloyerakis, a gendarme. Kaloyerakis lived with his family in a secluded house just outside Alikianos and was used to passing army patrols stopping at his home for water. He had no hesitation in opening the door that night when he heard knocking. The moment he unbolted the door the guerrillas burst in and shot him in the chest. His wife and four children were chased out of their home while some guerrillas prepared to blow it up and others plundered the rooms for food and clothing.

Concealed behind some trees nearby were two members of the newly formed local village defence force, the MAY. They were on duty that night guarding the bridge to the village and when they heard shots fired they moved cautiously in the direction of the shooting. They saw the guerrillas at the gendarme's home and immediately ran to the village to summon assistance. In a short time, the MAY returned in force and opened fire on the guerrillas just as they were making final preparations to detonate their explosives. The guerrillas returned fire briefly before making off into the hills with their booty. Kaloyerakis died of his wounds two hours later.

The deadline for the amnesty was drawing to a close. The authorities claimed it had been a great success but made it clear that a further extension to the time limit was out of the question and called on all the guerrillas to give themselves up without delay. With the encouragement of the authorities, dozens of letters from relatives of the guerrillas began to appear in the local press. All the letters were addressed to individuals in the mountains, urging them to surrender before the amnesty expired and threatening that family ties would be cut if they failed to do so. Without exception, the letter-writers added that they were not themselves members of any political organisation and had not been put under pressure by the authorities to advocate acceptance of the amnesty.

Among the letters to be published in the days before the amnesty expired was an appeal by Yanni Loupasis' two brothers pleading with him to accept the government amnesty or be disowned by them. Angelis Iliakis was urged by his father to surrender or be expelled from the family. Xenophon Kodonidis was called upon by his parents to give himself up or face eviction from the family, as was Sotiris Psarakis by his parents. A widowed mother threatened to disown her son and have nothing more to do with him if he did not accept the amnesty. But perhaps the most poignant of all the letters appealing to the guerrillas to surrender was one from a certain Marika telling her fiancé that if he did not give himself up she would break off their engagement.

Guerrillas continued to surrender and, to replace them, the communist leadership sent out small groups to various parts of Canea to recruit new members. Many of the guerrillas made for their native villages and persuaded young relatives and supporters to join them in the mountains. The muster was considered successful and the number of men with the guerrilla army gradually increased. At its peak the guerrilla army numbered three hundred.

But the increase in the number of men on Omalos caused extra supply problems. The stockpile of potatoes, their staple diet for the past two months, was running low and the guerrillas were facing a hungry winter. Their base was high in the mountains, far from the few friendly villages they could rely on for support. One way of obtaining fresh supplies of food was to steal more flocks and this in turn caused conflict with the villagers and an increasing loss of sympathy for the rebel movement.

An attempt to supplement the food stocks by attacking military supply trucks ended in failure. The guerrillas received a tip-off that the gendarme post at Kandanos was due to be re-supplied on a particular afternoon. According to their information the supply trucks would be accompanied by a few lightly armed guards. Just before midday the guerrillas prepared an ambush on the Kandanos road near Dromonero, and waited.

The Eagles of Crete

Later that afternoon two military trucks came into view. As the vehicles reached the ambush spot the guerrillas opened fire with machine guns and rifles from the heights above. The first truck was badly damaged and the men on board jumped down to the road, ran for cover and began to fire back at the unseen guerrillas on the hillside. The men from the second truck joined them but the driver, when he realised his engine was undamaged, reversed a short distance down the road. Out of sight of the guerrillas he turned the truck around and drove as fast as he could to the gendarme post at Voukolies for help.

The afternoon peace in the village was broken with the arrival of the truck driver, tooting his horn continuously to attract attention. With a screech of brakes he came to a halt outside the gendarme headquarters, jumped from the cab and spread the news of the ambush. Every available man was hurriedly mobilised and a relief column set off to the rescue.

The battle had been in progress for well over an hour by the time reinforcements arrived on the scene. Pinned down by the guerrillas, one of the gendarmes had been killed and another seriously wounded, but the escort had held out valiantly to deny the broken-down truck and its contents to the enemy. On the approach of the Voukolies garrison the guerrillas retreated. The gendarmes pursued them until they lost contact.

One dead guerrilla was found at the ambush spot but, as nobody recognised him, his body was taken back to Canea. He was later identified as Marios Stairopoulos by the aircraftsmen who were still being held at Firka Fortress, more than four months after their surrender. A known communist, Stairopoulos was from Athens and had been a member of ELAS on the mainland during the occupation. Among his possessions was a diary, which the authorities studied carefully.

Determined to put more pressure on the guerrillas, Gyparis announced that all the inhabitants of a village would be driven out of their homes if there was any suspicion that a single member of the community had given help of any kind to the guerrillas. Efforts to disarm the hill villagers were also increased.

Gyparis started by making an example of the village of Drakona. He arrived with his men early one morning in November, assembled the villagers in the square and ordered them to evacuate their homes forthwith. The majority of the inhabitants went to other villages where they had relatives; others had no alternative but to move into the mountains and live in caves. It was wintertime and bitterly cold. After six days Gyparis relented and allowed the villagers to return to their homes on condition they signed a public declaration of support for the government.

All the villagers returned to their homes and signed the declaration confirming that they would not in future give food and shelter to the guerrillas, including those who were natives of Drakona. They also promised to expel the guerrillas by force whenever they showed their faces and go to the aid of fellow villagers if they came under attack from the rebels. The villagers were warned that harsh measures would be taken against those who signed the declaration but failed to observe it.

The next to suffer were the inhabitants of three tiny hamlets south of Sassalos who were ordered to vacate their homes at short notice. As happened with Drakona, the villagers were allowed to return to their houses after agreeing to sign declarations of loyalty to the government. All adult males in Zourva, Prasses, Palea Roumata, Meskla and some of the smaller mountain villages made similar declarations.

Scarcely a week after the residents of Drakona signed their declaration, twenty guerrillas arrived in the village at 2 am. They made straight for the home of Emmanuel Sfingakis, a nationalist and former village president. A few months earlier Sfingakis had been attacked by two guerrillas who had beaten him half to death with their rifle butts. On this occasion the guerrillas burst into his home and accused him of giving information on guerrilla movements to the authorities and, despite his pleas of innocence, shot him in front of his family. They then set fire to his house and looted the home of another nationalist before they left, taking with them a mule, 50 sheep and a large quantity of olive oil.

A few nights later a small, heavily armed group of guerrillas attacked a prominent local nationalist in his home in Dris and shot him. The man's son and nephew, on a visit from Voukolies, attempted to resist the assailants but were also shot and killed. In the melee the wife grabbed at a guerrilla's machine gun in a desperate attempt to disarm him, but she only succeeded in spoiling his aim. The guerrilla shot himself in the leg and accidentally killed the woman's daughter. His comrades led the wounded guerrilla away from the village on a mule.

Two weeks later, on 17 December, the guerrillas carried out a large attack on Lakki in the early hours of the morning. Having received information that most of the gendarmes garrisoned in the village would be on leave, around eighty guerrillas left Omalos just after midnight and arrived on the outskirts of Lakki two hours before dawn.

The guerrilla attack was completely unexpected but the few remaining gendarmes and members of the local MAY, hastily rallied by their leaders, put up a determined resistance. Most of the guerrillas were prevented from entering the village but a small, determined band, well armed with machine guns and grenades, eventually managed to fight its way through the defenders and capture the gendarme post. After seizing all the files and documents, they set the building on fire and withdrew, just as the sun was rising.

No casualties were suffered by the guerrillas but one member of the MAY was killed and another wounded. Without hesitation, the MAY fell in and set off in pursuit, confident that they would catch up with and surprise the guerrillas before they reached Omalos.

The guerrillas had anticipated a pursuit and carefully prepared an ambush two kilometres outside the village. When the guerrillas spotted the MAY coming along the track in a careless rush, they opened fire, killing two of them. There was no further pursuit. Soon after this raid, the authorities established a small army garrison of one platoon in two old Turkish towers above Lakki.

Towards the end of 1947, roadblocks began to reappear in western Crete at Kakopetros and, days later, a few kilometres from Paleohora. Buses were held up and passengers robbed, and two members of the MAY were killed in pursuit of those responsible. The guerrillas then vanished without trace.

Another band of eight men under Zacharias Bandourakis, a cousin of the late guerrilla leader, cut down the telephone wires outside Drapanias and, as it grew dark, set up a roadblock nearby. Soon two cars were spotted coming from the direction of Canea. Both vehicles were stopped and the seven male passengers ordered out and searched. A large sum of money was found on the men and immediately pocketed by the guerrillas.

All the men were taken hostage but a couple of hours later five of them were released. The guerrillas then split up, with four of the men heading south; Bandourakis and his three remaining followers and the two hostages went north. Those with Bandourakis made their way along the coast below Ravdouha and spent what was left of the night at a small chapel by the sea. Early the following morning they were spotted by a shepherd who ran off without the guerrillas seeing him and informed the authorities of their whereabouts.

Two platoons of soldiers, gendarme patrols and the local MAY had been combing the area in the search for the guerrillas for half the night. When informed of their location, the search parties moved quickly to encircle their quarry. The small chapel was hemmed in between precipitous cliffs and the sea and later that morning the guerrillas realised they were surrounded.

The government forces had the advantage of superior numbers and firepower but could make no headway against the guerrillas who put up stubborn resistance for the whole of that day. By dusk, three soldiers, one gendarme and two of the MAY had been wounded. However, the guerrillas were very low on ammunition and unable to prevent a gendarme getting close enough to hurl several grenades directly at them.

After a long period of complete silence, the soldiers and gendarmes approached the rebel position. They found three dead guerrillas and Bandourakis, seriously wounded in the leg and bleeding profusely. The gendarmes put Bandourakis on a mule to take him to Kastelli clinic for treatment but he died on the journey.

The Eagles of Crete

A week after the battle below Ravdouha a headless body was washed up on a nearby beach. It was later confirmed to be that of one of the hostages taken by Zacharias Bandourakis' band.

Chapter 7
Government Minister Ambushed

All gendarmes garrisoned in Kalives were given generous leave for the New Year holiday and, in their absence, a handful of guerrillas tied explosives to the bridge outside the village. The detonation was heard far and wide and a large hole was made in the bridge itself. Although the foundations remained in place they were badly damaged and traffic across the bridge was stopped for several weeks.

Two days after the explosion several men were arrested in Kalives. The police announced that certain locals had known of the plan to blow up the bridge and had done nothing to prevent it. Others had seen guerrillas in the area on the night of its demolition and had not informed the authorities. For failing to prevent the destruction of the bridge, the villagers of Kalives, Gavalohori, Plaka and Kokkino Horio were informed that they would have to pay for its repair. The eventual bill came to thirty million drachmas.

Throughout January 1948, guerrillas raided villages for food, targeting areas where there were no gendarme posts. In one village there were casualties. Loulos was surrounded by guerrillas who opened fire indiscriminately, wounding three children, and threw sticks of dynamite, killing two teenage girls. Houses were ransacked, food was loaded onto mules and sheep were rounded up and driven off by the guerrillas. The villagers offered no resistance.

Raids to obtain food were also made on Nea Roumata, Voutas and Thimia, where guerrillas entered a house on the edge of the tiny village owned by a member of the MAY. The guerrillas plundered the house and took the man's rifle, donkey, fifteen sheep, and a slaughtered pig with them back to the mountains.

Patrols of gendarmes, supported by the MAY, were regularly out searching for the elusive guerrillas and met with the occasional success. One guerrilla was shot and killed one night at Koukounara when he ran away from a gendarme patrol; and a former guerrilla who had received an amnesty was killed in Palea Roumata by the MAY.

Dimitri Ledakis, who ran messages between guerrilla bands, was wounded by a gendarme patrol as he fled from Varipetro. Another guerrilla, Spiro Blazakis, was found hiding in Ramni and chased by gendarmes. Although wounded slightly in the leg, Blazakis escaped by stealing a horse and riding down to the coast. Later that day the gendarme patrol came across an armed man and shot him. They realised they had made a tragic mistake when the dead man was identified as a member of the local MAY who had been out hunting.

A MAY patrol challenged five men they spotted near Galatas and captured one of them as they ran off. At first the man claimed he was out late laying traps for hares but eventually admitted that he was a former guerrilla who had surrendered some time ago and been granted his freedom in return for signing a declaration of repentance. The man agreed to take the MAY to his comrades' hide-out but on the way there he tried to escape in the darkness. He was shot and taken to hospital seriously wounded.

By the end of January, the deep snow and cold weather had driven nearly all of the guerrillas from their main base on Omalos to the hill villages. A few small groups had remained in the mountains and one of these had taken to hiding in some ruined farm buildings near to Fokies, where Manoli Bandourakis and his men had been ambushed.

One foggy morning, the guerrillas observed a patrol heading in the direction of their hideout. The guerrillas concealed themselves and waited for the patrol to pass by, but when it became obvious the gendarmes intended to enter the buildings they opened fire. One of the first shots hit the MAY leader in the stomach. His comrades hastily took cover and for twenty minutes there was an exchange of fire, followed by complete silence from the farm buildings. Taking full advantage of the poor visibility, the guerrillas had slipped away

The gendarmes made a close search of the buildings and found a large patch of blood but no body. A young guerrilla had been seriously wounded but had been helped away by his companions. He died in the mountains a few days later. The only casualty suffered by the patrol was the MAY leader, a prominent citizen of Lakki, who was taken to Canea and after surgery made a full recovery.

A week later, a MAY unit on its way from Therisso to Meskla came across three guerrillas just outside Meskla cemetery. The guerrillas were sitting in an olive grove, eating their lunch of bread and cheese, and were taken unawares by the patrol. Before they had a chance to reach for their rifles, the MAY opened fire, killing one of the guerrillas and capturing another; the third made a run for it and escaped.

The captured man was recognised as Panayiotis Tsamantis, the brother of the deputy leader of the guerrilla army. Nobody knew the identity of the dead guerrilla, who was found to be in possession of a false identity document and it was to be several days before the authorities were able to name him as one of Podias' men from eastern Crete. Shortly after Tsamantis was arrested, his mother was taken into custody and charged with sheltering guerrillas.

At the beginning of February 1948, around 60 guerrillas gathered at the shepherds' huts at Voulisma in the mountains above Zourva. Reports of the presence of large numbers of guerrillas in one place soon reached Colonel Frangiadakis in Canea after a patrol on the track between Therisso and Zourva was forced to retreat when it came under fire from guerrillas hiding behind boulders on the hillside above.

Colonel Frangiadakis arrived in Therisso with reinforcements to take personal charge of the developing military operation. The large number of guerrillas had been pinpointed and Frangiadakis was confident that, with the help of the misty weather, he would be able to surround the guerrillas and force them to give battle. He divided his men, sending half of them to the rear of the guerrillas; the rest of his troops were to make a frontal assault on their positions.

To Frangiadakis' dismay, the guerrillas dispersed as soon as the attack started. Some of them made off towards the east, but most headed south into the higher mountains. Frangiadakis' men pursued the guerrillas for the rest of that day, firing mortars whenever they spotted the enemy in the distance; the guerrillas replied with machine-gun fire. The deserted shepherds' huts at Voulisma were captured and destroyed to prevent their future use by the enemy. All that the soldiers found at the huts was a large cauldron of lentil soup, which they overturned and poured into the ground.

That night the soldiers bivouacked in the mountains and returned to the attack the following morning. By this time the guerrillas had split into even smaller groups and gone deeper into the mountains. The soldiers continued their pursuit, some of them climbing mountain peaks to scan the horizon for signs of the enemy.

Gunfire could be heard south of Zourva all day but a thick mist fell and heavy rain made it easy for the guerrillas to move around unseen. That night they finally gave their pursuers the slip. Faced with bad weather, the soldiers had no option but to give up their search and return to their base. One soldier had been slightly wounded but no other casualties were suffered by either side in the two days of skirmishing.

On 10 February 1948, a large band of guerrillas prepared to ambush the bus on the deserted mountain road between Lakki and Fournes on a bend where the bus would have to slow down. When the bus came into view the guerrillas, guns raised, stepped into the road and signalled the driver to stop. Surrounded by armed men on all sides, the driver did as he was bidden.

As usual, there were several villagers on the bus that morning but there were also ten of the soldiers from the recently established garrison post above the village. Most of the soldiers were on leave and only three or four of them were armed. The guerrillas ordered all the passengers to leave their bags and guns on their seats and to get off the bus. Everybody did as they were told and the guerrillas gave the bus a thorough search. After taking all the weapons, they allowed the villagers to get back on the bus and continue their journey to Canea. The soldiers, however, they kept with them, and as soon as the bus was out of sight, they marched their prisoners off into the mountains.

The Eagles of Crete

Patrols were dispatched to search for the soldiers and their captors but were hampered by bad weather. Two days later, several relatives of guerrillas were arrested in Orthouni and Karanos and were warned they faced severe penalties if the abducted soldiers were not released. Representatives were hurriedly chosen by the villagers to find the guerrillas and plead with them for the release of their captives.

Later that day the village representatives made contact with the guerrillas on the Omalos Plateau. While they had been held captive, the soldiers had been subjected to a great deal of propaganda, with constant demands that they desert their unit and throw in their lot with the guerrilla army. All the rebel appeals had fallen on deaf ears and the villagers had little difficulty in persuading the guerrillas to release the soldiers.

As darkness fell, the soldiers were told to hand over their uniforms and boots and were then taken down the track leading to Agia Irini and released. On their arrival in Agia Irini the sympathetic villagers took them into their homes. Old clothing and footwear were found for them as the soldiers recounted the story of their abduction. The authorities were informed of their release and the following day the soldiers made their way to Canea.

Just over a week later, 40 well-armed guerrillas descended on Orthouni. The village was occupied and two villagers were seized from their homes and led up to Omalos. On the plateau, the prisoners, a man and an elderly widow, were given a trial by a Guerrilla Court. Both were accused of giving information on the guerrilla movements to the authorities. At the end of the brief trial both prisoners were found guilty and executed.

A short time afterwards, the guerrillas seized two shepherds, one from Orthouni and the other from Kares, as they pastured their flocks. The men and their animals were taken to Omalos and the shepherds were put before the same court and found guilty of informing on the guerrillas to the authorities. They were executed on the plateau the same day.

On March 1, a dozen guerrillas once again ambushed the bus from Lakki as it made its way down the narrow mountain road to

Fournes. The driver - the same driver who had been held up less than three weeks earlier - stopped immediately he spotted the armed men standing in the road. He and the fourteen passengers, all civilians, were ordered from the bus and searched for money and weapons. This time, instead of letting the villagers continue their journey, as they had previously, the guerrillas burnt the bus and took the driver and passengers with them to Askordalos, where other guerrillas were waiting.

In Askordalos, the guerrillas released eight of the passengers but kept the remaining six and the driver, all believed to be nationalists, and set off towards Omalos. Before they had gone far, one of the hostages managed to escape and hide in a cypress tree. The guerrillas searched for their escaped prisoner briefly but, finding no sign of him, continued on their way. When the coast was clear, the man came out of hiding and made for the gendarme post at Alikianos.

News of the ambush and abductions soon reached Lakki and a crowd of angry villagers gathered in the square to discuss what action they should take. Feelings were running high and relatives of guerrillas and suspected communist sympathisers in Lakki were apprehended by locals. In all, the nationalists seized a total of fifteen men. The families of the men were warned that these hostages would be executed if the passengers abducted from the bus were not released immediately. The authorities made no move to interfere and when the guerrillas on Omalos heard of the arrests in Lakki they released the passengers and allowed them to return to their homes. On their arrival back in Lakki, the fifteen hostages held by the nationalists were released.

As the weather improved, two large bands of guerrillas, totalling 80 men, left the Omalos Plateau and headed for the villages in the west. Joseph Bitzanakis led one group to Voutas while *Kapetan* George led the other to the Elos area, where he had previously been based. Their intention was to recruit as many villagers as they could into the guerrilla army.

Early one morning, a runner came to *Kapetan* George with the news that a gendarme patrol was heading his way. Rather than make a run for it, *Kapetan* George planned an ambush and posted his men above the track the gendarmes were taking.

At the last moment the guerrillas lost the element of surprise when one of their number opened fire too early. The gendarmes took cover and, despite being outnumbered, successfully held off the guerrillas for some time. The noise of the battle reached nearby villages and word of the ambush soon spread. MAY units and gendarme reinforcements were mobilised in Topolia and dispatched by truck to Elos. As soon as they arrived the guerrillas began to retreat southwards, planning to join forces with their comrades in Voutas. Gendarme reinforcements from Kastelli set out by truck for Elos.

Meanwhile, on Bitzanakis' arrival in Voutas, the village was declared a liberated area. A day of feasting was planned and the village was decorated with laurel and myrtle and communist slogans were daubed on the walls of all the houses. Local women made pastries and sweetmeats and sheep and goats were killed and made ready for barbecue.

News of the guerrillas in Voutas soon reached Paleohora. Lt Lazopoulos immediately set off to engage them with all the men under his command and as he moved through the villages was joined by local volunteers. At the same time, gendarmes and MAY began to move towards Voutas from Kandanos.

Later that afternoon, Bitzanakis got wind of the approaching enemy force. He and his men immediately fled the village, planning to escape to the south, but they had not gone far before they ran into an army patrol. Unable to give the soldiers the slip, the guerrillas were forced to give battle. After a time, they managed to disengage without loss and retreat towards Chrissoskalitissa.

Kapetan George's band also came under intense pressure from the MAY and gendarmes pursuing them and, faced with the enemy on three sides, was forced to flee westward. The band split into smaller groups. Three guerrillas, discovered hiding in a small ravine, were surrounded and killed and four others were captured in a separate encounter but the rest made good their escape and joined up with Bitzanakis and his men.

With the sea at their backs, the guerrillas hid in caves, ravines and the forested hillsides, waiting for the hunt for them to die down. The weather was good, and when night came there was a full moon to aid the government troops in their search. However, after two days spent combing the area, no further trace of the guerrillas was found and the search parties were called off and ordered back to their bases.

Government forces had suffered no losses, and Lt Lazopoulos was full of praise for the enthusiasm with which the villagers had spontaneously joined him. On his way back to Paleohora, he stopped at Voutas and arrested 34 women and 24 men, on the grounds that they were related to guerrillas or were suspected of aiding them. One villager found to be in possession of a large quantity of medical supplies was about to be arrested when he made a run for it and was shot down before he could reach the safety of the olive groves.

Shortage of food led many guerrillas to desert. The leadership was unable to guarantee that new recruits would be fed and was thus unable to increase the number of men in the ranks of their guerrilla army. Rebel supporters were hard-pressed by the increasing numbers of patrols, and supplies from the villages were decreasing. Not surprisingly, thefts of flocks and herds carried out by the guerrillas made them unpopular with the local shepherds.

One of their sources of supply came from Canea town itself. For a time, some of the money that had fallen into the hands of the guerrillas had been used to buy food which was then transported to the mountains. This particular arrangement was brought to an end following a tip-off from a suspicious shopkeeper to the police. A villager from Prasses, who had come into town one morning, had bought an inordinate amount of food and the incredulous shopkeeper immediately reported the matter to the police.

By the time the police took action the afternoon bus for Prasses had already left town. The police set off in pursuit and caught up with the bus in the middle of the countryside. The shopkeeper's customer was soon identified and arrested. An accomplice and the bus driver were also taken into custody and sacks of cereals and beans were confiscated.

Within days the authorities had taken steps to prevent the guerrillas obtaining provisions from the town. In future, citizens were liable to be arrested on the spot if found to be in possession of large amounts of food or medical supplies. A police permit was required for those wishing to purchase more than was considered necessary for the immediate needs of themselves and their families. Shopkeepers were forbidden to sell vast quantities of food to a single customer and those transporting food throughout the countryside had to register with the police, giving details of the amounts they were carrying and their destination.

At the same time citizens were reminded that it was an offence to donate money to the guerrillas, even if the donations were made under duress. That very week, the new president of Palea Roumata reported to the gendarmerie that guerrillas had demanded he collect money from the villagers on their behalf. The guerrillas had arrived at his home one night and told him they would return at a later date to collect the cash. As they left they gave stern warning of what would happen if the money were not ready when they came back. It had long been illegal to make financial donations to the KKE and the head of the gendarmerie announced that in future all those who donated money to the guerrillas would be regarded as supporters of the rebel movement and treated accordingly.

Late at night on 10 March, a large armed body left Omalos and took a minor path down to Epanohori. As quietly as possible, two of the guerrillas went to the home of a nationalist and knocked at his door. When the man opened it he was seized by the guerrillas and taken to where their comrades were waiting.

The nationalist was then told to accompany the guerrillas to the home of his friend, Vangelis Protopapadakis. The nationalist did as he was ordered and Protopapadakis, without the slightest suspicion, unbarred his door to his old friend. Immediately he did so he was grabbed and the guerrillas poured into his home. In complete silence they took his radio and all the food and clothing they could find. After setting fire to the house, the guerrillas left the village as silently as they had arrived, taking their two hostages with them.

Later that night the nationalist was released. The fate of Protopapadakis remained unknown until the following day when his mother, on her way to Omalos to plead for her son's release, came across his decapitated body on the path just outside the village of Agia Irini.

One night a week later, a member of the local MAY in Perivolia had a lucky escape when guerrillas dressed in army uniforms knocked at his door and asked for water. The man smelt a rat and instead of opening the door fired above the heads of the men outside. A few shots were exchanged but the guerrillas soon withdrew. On their way back to the mountains they attacked another member of the MAY in his home in Mournies. On this occasion they were more successful, wounding both the man and his son.

Around the same time, two members of the MAY from Pemonia were shot and killed by men waiting in ambush for them when they arrived to guard a bridge for the night. In another attack, one of the six soldiers guarding Agia reservoir was shot in the chest and seriously wounded by an unseen sniper.

Sophocles Venizelos had been Prime Minister for two weeks in the Greek government-in-exile in April 1944. In 1948 he was serving as a minister in the coalition government of Themistocles Sophoulis. Venizelos was unpopular with some of his fellow Cretans because he had done nothing to prevent young Cretan conscripts being sent to the mainland where civil war was raging. He was particularly unpopular with the communists in Crete on account of his strong support for Gyparis.

For some time the Kyrix newspaper, owned by the Liberal MP, Constantine Mitsotakis, had been reminding its readers of the forthcoming visit of Sophocles Venizelos, who was due in Canea for a commemoration service at his father's grave on Akrotiri. Prime Minister Sophoulis was to arrive in Souda by warship on the same day. Details

The Eagles of Crete

of Venizelos' itinerary were given out in advance: he would land at Heraklion airport and meet various political leaders before continuing his journey to Canea by road. This information was all the guerrillas needed to know.

An ambush spot was chosen by the guerrillas on the main road near Maheri. On more than one occasion the authorities had declared this area to be free of guerrillas, and it is said that when Venizelos checked with Gyparis before the journey that the route was safe he was told it was "as peaceful as Switzerland".

Christos Boloudakis, known as *Kapetan* Tovaris (*tovaris* being the Russian word for comrade), was put in charge of fifteen specially selected sharpshooters, who were to ambush Venizelos. There were to be two other bands, with around twenty men in each, to guard the flanks of Boloudakis' ambush party and cover its retreat.

All the guerrillas involved in the ambush moved down from Omalos to Drakona at night and late the following day made for Kares, where they were given an enthusiastic reception. At sunset, the guerrillas in the ambush party descended to the hill above Maheri, arriving just after midnight.

Smoking and talking was forbidden and the men waited in total silence with their rations of bread and water. They had taken up position 700 metres from the road but the men were all crack shots and were convinced they would hit their target when Venizelos appeared.

Venizelos left Heraklion at 9 am on the morning of 19 March. He was accompanied by Petrakageorgis, the MP for Heraklion, and the MPs for Lasithi and Rethymnon. Constantine Mitsotakis and Yanni Bandouvas were among the many other dignitaries with him. The journey to Rethymnon took four hours, the motorcade stopping in several villages along the way to receive a warm welcome from the inhabitants.

In Rethymnon, Venizelos made a speech that was greeted with great applause. After lunch, he and his entourage set off for Georgioupolis, and were met by Colonel Frangiadakis and Gyparis. Bandouvas and several of the politicians from Heraklion and Rethymnon left Venizelos at this point. Venizelos set out for Neo Horio, where a large crowd was awaiting him.

It was just after 5 pm when Venizelos' convoy of a dozen cars and jeeps came into view of the guerrillas hiding above Maheri. As soon as it reached the point in the road targeted by the guerrillas, they opened fire. Most of the vehicles received direct hits in the first burst of gunfire and those on board leapt out and took cover in a shallow ditch by the side of the road. The armed men with Venizelos returned fire but were pinned down by shots coming from the men who were guarding the ambush party's flanks.

It was half an hour before MAY units from nearby villages came to the assistance of the beleaguered party. The guerrillas, on the approach of the MAY, retreated towards Ramni. They were pursued until midnight but all escaped into the mountains.

In spite of the number of shots fired at them, only two of Venizelos' party had suffered injury. Venizelos' driver had been hit in the hip and leg and was taken directly to hospital, where he made a full recovery. Petrakageorgis was badly cut in the face by fragments of sharp stone that had been thrown up by the gunfire. Except for these two men the only harm done was to the dignity of the politicians who, in their smart suits, had had to jump into the ditch to seek safety and remain there, face down in the dust, until the shooting had stopped.

As soon as it was considered safe to do so, Venizelos continued his journey to Canea. He stopped briefly in Neo Horio to reassure the waiting crowd and then proceeded to town. News of the attack had already spread and sympathetic villagers lined his route to greet him. On arrival in Canea, Venizelos confirmed that he intended to fulfil his programme as planned and remain in Canea for a further three days.

Gyparis had not accompanied Venizelos on the final leg of his journey but had stayed behind and joined in the pursuit of the guerrillas. In Ramni he ordered two houses to be burnt and arrested the village priest, who was suspected of aiding the guerrillas.

A few days later a letter, signed by fifty-three male inhabitants of Maheri, was published in the local paper, condemning the attack on Venizelos and confirming that the whole village was one hundred per cent on the side of law and order. The Ramni priest was released after signing a public declaration that he supported the rightful authorities and giving his word that he had never provided the guerrillas with any kind of assistance.

An enquiry in Athens cleared the local military authorities of any blame over the attack, in particular their failure to guard the Canea-Rethymnon road on the day of the ambush. Nevertheless, Colonel Frangiadakis was replaced by Lt Colonel George Vardoulakis, a Cretan from Anopolis, who was given sole military command in the war against the communists. Gyparis henceforth devoted himself to a successful political career.

Another 150 gendarmes who had recently completed their training on the mainland were immediately posted to Crete. These gendarme reinforcements had been requested by the local MPs for some time but it was only after being ambushed that Venizelos personally intervened to persuade the Athens government to strengthen the gendarmerie on the island. The arrival of this new battalion and the appointment of Vardoulakis as military commander finally signalled the beginning of the end for the guerrilla army.

Within a week of the arrival of the gendarme reinforcements, the authorities reported the deaths of two guerrillas in unconnected incidents near Voutas. One young guerrilla was spotted by a patrol and took refuge in a church outside Sarakina. Called upon to surrender he shot at the gendarmes and was killed when they returned fire. Later that day an ELAS veteran was ambushed near his native village of Kamaria. A few days later, nineteen guerrillas from the Voutas area surrendered to the authorities with their weapons.

In Apokoronas, a mixed patrol of gendarmes and soldiers were on their way to Kokkino Horio early one morning when they spotted two armed men in the distance. The men refused to stop when ordered to and opened fire on the patrol. After a brief exchange of shots the two men were killed. They were identified as Nikos Blazakis of Gavalohori and George Sergakis of Drapanos. Blazakis had only been with the guerrillas for a few weeks, having joined his elder brother, Spiro, in the mountains that winter. The patrol continued its search for other guerrillas in the area and came across a cave near Kokkino Horio that was being used as a hide-out. A cache of ammunition was discovered and a large quantity of food, some of it cooked and ready to eat, was destroyed.

On 1 April, eleven guerrillas set up a roadblock at Messavlia and halted the bus from Paleohora to Canea. After checking the identity cards of the passengers, the guerrillas took two of them hostage. The bus was allowed to continue on its journey and the guerrillas set off with their hostages to Milonou.

Army patrols and units of MAY moved against Milonou from different directions and the guerrillas were eventually cornered that afternoon by an army patrol that had come from Sassalos. In the confusion of the long gun battle that followed, the two hostages managed to escape. The guerrillas held off the patrol for some time and as soon as it grew dark they made their getaway, taking a wounded comrade with them and leaving behind the dead body of another.

A few days later three armed men were spotted near Milonou by a MAY patrol. The men were fired upon when they made a run for it and one of them, a guerrilla from Sassalos, was killed by the opening burst of gunfire. It soon began to rain heavily and although a careful search was made of the area, no trace of the other two men was found.

The MAY and an army patrol advanced to Sassalos, where the home of Nikolaos Xeroyannakis, a *kapetan* with the guerrillas, was set on fire. Villagers were questioned about guerrilla movements in the area and Yanni Koutoulakis, who had a young relative with the guerrillas in the mountains, was placed under arrest. According to the official account of the incident, 72-year-old Koutoulakis is said to have resisted and was shot dead as he attempted to escape.

A week later two important communists were captured just outside Canea when a gendarme patrol and a MAY unit attempted to carry out a house-to-house search in Perivolia. As they were about to enter a particular building, a man came out from behind some bushes and fired upon the gendarmes. The patrol returned fire and the armed man immediately threw down his pistol and surrendered. He was quickly identified by members of the MAY as Dimitri Ledakis, a messenger for the guerrillas from nearby Varipetro.

The Eagles of Crete

The gendarmes resumed their search and found a man hiding in the yard of the house they had been about to enter before Ledakis opened fire on them. The man was armed with a German machine gun and several grenades but surrendered the moment he was discovered. The second prisoner identified himself as George Papayannakis, a leading member of the KKE organisation in Canea. Both men were in possession of KKE literature and Papayannakis had a diary and notebook with him that suggested he was in charge of the guerrilla commissariat.

The family in whose home Papayannakis had taken shelter was arrested, along with three relatives. All the captives were ordered to march the short distance into Canea. As news of the arrests spread, a crowd began to line the streets and many of the townspeople followed the prisoners right up to the gates of Firka jail.

The guerrillas on the Omalos Plateau were coming under mounting pressure from government patrols. Movement to and from the plateau was becoming more difficult as small groups were attacked and larger ones shadowed. Only by moving at night were the guerrillas successfully able to dodge their pursuers.

In early April, an armed party of guerrillas left Omalos during the night and made its way down the mountainside on steep, slippery goat paths to Epanohori. All was quiet as they moved into the village unobserved.

Three houses were set alight but before the guerrillas could do more damage, they came under intense fire. The small gendarme post recently established in the village had been reinforced, without the guerrillas' knowledge, the previous day. Fearing that their plans had been betrayed and disconcerted by the large number of gendarmes and local MAY, the guerrillas were forced to flee the village. Their retreat up the steep hillside was laboriously slow and they had to crawl much of the way to avoid giving the defenders a clear target.

There was only one casualty: Epimenidis Athanasakis, from Sassalos. Seriously wounded in the attack, he was carried back to Omalos by his comrades, but died on the way. In the morning Athanasakis was laid to rest in a shallow grave on the plateau. His seventeen-year-old sister, Xenoula, had left home to join her brother in the mountains a few weeks earlier. When she learnt of her brother's death she was inconsolable.

Chapter 8
The Battle in the Samaria Gorge

Less than a month after the attack on Venizelos, all the guerrillas were assembled once again on the Omalos. They were badly in need of a victory of some sort. Information that seemed to guarantee a successful operation soon came their way.

Stelios Fitourakis was one of the national servicemen based at Lakki. For some time he had been considering defecting to the guerrillas and one weekend, while visiting his parents in Therisso, had made contact with the rebels. Fitourakis was questioned at length over the strength of the Lakki garrison, details of sentry movements, and the garrison routine. It was agreed that Fitourakis would return to Lakki and, on the next full moon, the guerrillas would attack in strength and capture the guard post.

As soon as it grew dark on the evening of 17 April, 150 guerrillas moved down the mountain towards Lakki. Above the village the guerrillas split into two groups: one was to make the attack on the army guard post, south-west of Lakki, and the other was to prevent the arrival of reinforcements. The garrison was quartered in two old Turkish towers on Savoure hill and the attack was planned to take place a few minutes after the guard changed at midnight.

The attack on the upper tower, which housed twenty soldiers, was a complete success. A few shots were fired to terrify the guard and the post was taken without a fight. For some reason, the assault on the lower tower was delayed and the ten soldiers stationed there, alerted by the nearby shooting, escaped into the village. The guerrillas lost no time in ransacking the two towers and carrying off everything they could take with them. Their booty included three stens, fifteen rifles, a mortar, ammunition and all the blankets, food and clothing.

The soldiers from the lower tower raised the alarm in Lakki. Members of the local MAY and gendarmes quickly mobilised and set off to rescue the captive soldiers but were stopped in their tracks by a volley of rifle fire from the guerrillas waiting outside the village. A battle broke out and continued for two hours. Despite using mortars, the gendarmes could not disperse the rebels, who stood firm and gave their comrades plenty of time to retreat to Omalos with their booty and prisoners.

Two of the soldiers from the lower fort were wounded in the battle, one fatally. When the guerrillas withdrew, traces of blood were found, suggesting that at least one guerrilla had been seriously wounded. No attempt was made to pursue the large guerrilla band that night.

Fitourakis had joined the guerrillas immediately the upper fort fell. He was the only soldier allowed to retain his weapon and on the march up to Omalos urged his fellow servicemen to throw in their lot with the guerrillas. His appeals fell on deaf ears and the nineteen captives walked in silence to the plateau.

Later that morning, *Kapetan* Mihali addressed the soldiers but all of his efforts to persuade them to join the guerrillas failed. Orders were given for the commander, Lt Yanni Patsidiotis, to be detained and for the two sergeants and sixteen men to be released. Before they left, their boots and uniforms were taken and in exchange they were given the tattered clothes that some of the guerrillas had been wearing. Barefoot, the soldiers made their way back to Lakki.

On arrival in the village, the two sergeants were arrested and sent to Canea. A short time later they were put on trial, accused of cowardice and of failing to defend their post. When the case was heard, evidence was presented that Fitourakis had been in league with the guerrillas from the beginning and the two men were acquitted.

Their commanding officer was not so fortunate. Patsidiotis was accused of collaborating with the Germans during the occupation and put on trial by the guerrillas. Found guilty, the lieutenant was taken to the edge of the Samaria Gorge and beheaded. The executioner threw the body and head into the gorge, hundreds of metres below.

The Eagles of Crete

In anticipation of a raid on their base, the guerrillas split up, with many making for distant parts of the prefecture. Around 70 guerrillas sought refuge in the Samaria Gorge.

Later that morning, the army arrived on Omalos in force. No trace was found of the guerrillas but a recently dug grave was discovered and the body of a young man who had been shot in the chest was unearthed. This confirmed suspicions that at least one guerrilla had been killed in the battle the previous night.

Several army patrols and units of MAY made their way through the mountains from different directions and converged on the Omalos Plateau. Colonel Vardoulakis arrived at the gorge entrance at Xyloskalo with a force of gendarmes to take personal charge of the search. For three days the patrols swept the area. Brief contact was made with guerrillas on the western slopes of Mount Psilaphi and a longer battle took place on the eastern side of the gorge after the guerrillas ambushed a gendarme patrol at Potamos, killing one gendarme and wounding another.

It was clear to Vardoulakis and his senior officers that a large number of guerrillas had taken refuge in the Samaria Gorge and after long consideration the decision was taken to enter the gorge and force a confrontation. Throughout Cretan history, Samaria had been a safe haven for fugitives and the remote gorge provided dozens of suitable hiding places and many areas where determined defenders could set lethal ambushes. The guerrillas regarded the gorge as impregnable; Vardoulakis ordered his men to move forward slowly and cautiously and search all caves meticulously.

The guerrillas had made their camp in the middle of the gorge, just north of the village of Samaria. News of the persistent patrols had reached them and a young messenger from Zourva had been unable to leave the gorge owing to the large number of soldiers and gendarmes in the mountains.

Among those in the gorge were the KKE Secretary, George Tsitilos, and *Kapetan* Tsamantis. As an incursion into the gorge was anticipated, a meeting of all the guerrillas was held, at which there was general agreement that they should avoid a battle, and either hide or attempt to break out of the gorge at night.

The leaders and female guerrillas set off to find secure hiding places to the east of their camp while a large group of guerrillas, determined to break out of the gorge, made for the tiny church of Agios Nikolaos. During the day they hid from the search parties and as soon as it grew dark started to make their way, slowly and silently, towards the gorge exit at Poria.

Throughout the night they continued their climb, carefully picking their way up the mountainside. The moonlight helped them in their ascent but there was a bitterly cold north wind blowing. As they approached Poria they got down on all fours and crawled forward. There was no sign of any sentries guarding the path's exit from the gorge but the guerrillas stopped for a few minutes and listened. Faint voices could be heard in the distance so the guerrillas inched their way forward. Eventually they were able to make out the figures of several gendarmes who had taken shelter in and around a shepherd's hut, where they had lit a large fire.

The guerrillas crawled out of the gorge, keeping to the hillside above Poria and giving the shepherd's hut a wide berth. When they had put some distance between themselves and the gendarmes they hurried across some patches of snow and scattered into the mountains. In the morning the gendarmes discovered the guerrillas' footprints in the snow and realised that a large number of men had escaped from the gorge that night while the sentries had been warming themselves by the fire.

With no resistance offered, Vardoulakis captured the guerrilla camp in Samaria Gorge without difficulty. The mortar and three stens taken from the Lakki garrison were found in the camp together with possessions and documents left behind by the guerrillas.

The guerrillas had been surviving on a diet of sheep and goat and there were animal bones and goatskins all around the camp. A cow was discovered nearby with its stomach cut open and there were flies everywhere. In the cooking area, beneath a large cypress tree, some pieces of boiled meat were found floating in oil in old tins. Other dirty, greasy cans had been used for collecting drinking water.

Vardoulakis had no intention of remaining in the gorge and the order to pull out was given as soon as the vicinity of the camp had been searched. The surviving animals were driven from the gorge and returned to their rightful owners in the villages. All the property that could not be taken out of the gorge was destroyed on the spot.

As Easter drew near, around 100 guerrillas gathered together near a spring, high in the mountains above Zourva. Clouds were low and visibility poor. Lookouts were posted but, given the weather conditions, were lax and many guerrillas expected the military to be on leave for the Easter period. No truce had been declared but the guerrillas were looking forward to a period of relaxation. Sheep and goats had been skinned ready to cook and several of the guerrillas had washed clothes and hung them out to dry.

Early on Easter Friday morning, a combined force of gendarmes and MAY, numbering a hundred men, arrived in Zourva and set off on patrol through the mountains. Their route was to take them via the spring at which the guerrillas were camped.

That afternoon, many of the guerrillas were sitting around, sprawled under the trees, smoking and chatting together. Some were dozing and others were washing their hair at the spring when an advance party of gendarmes appeared out of the mist. Both sides were taken completely by surprise. The gendarmes retreated and took cover; several of the guerrillas were unable at first to find their weapons but firing broke out from both sides as gendarme reinforcements arrived and the guerrillas recovered from their confusion.

The guerrillas had chosen a strong position for their camp and put up a successful defence for three hours, using mortar fire to keep the gendarmes at bay. Early in the evening they stopped firing and withdrew. The gendarmes took control of the guerrilla camp, abandoned except for some male and female clothing that was hanging up to dry. There were patches of blood on the rocks, suggesting that at least one of the guerrillas had been wounded.

For the rest of the day the gendarmes and the MAY hunted for the guerrillas, and later that evening caught up with them and forced them to give battle once again. When night fell the guerrillas slipped away and went deeper into the mountains. That night they split up into small groups and scattered in different directions. By the end of the following day the government forces, having found no further trace of the guerrillas, gave up the search and returned to their barracks.

In early May, Mihali Yerakakis, a veteran of several major actions, including the raid on Georgioupolis and the attack on Venizelos, was betrayed and killed. Yerakakis had gone to the hut of a cheese-maker, by the name of Grivas, to ask for something to eat. Yerakakis had no reason to be suspicious as the cheese-maker had often fed him in the past and after the meal he told Grivas that he would return the following day. As soon as Yerakakis had gone, Grivas sent a boy to the MAY at Agii Pandes, informing them that Yerakakis was in the area alone and would be at his hut the next day. On learning of Yerakakis' whereabouts a dozen members of the MAY hurried to Grivas' hut and prepared an ambush, and when the unsuspecting guerrilla returned he was shot down and killed.

News of this treachery spread rapidly through the mountains. All the guerrillas were incensed at the loss of their loyal comrade and Christos Boloudakis was dispatched to Grivas' hut with a force of 50 men. Grivas, the four shepherds with him, their combined herds of 700 goats and all their cheese and cheese-making equipment were seized and taken into the mountains.

Two of the shepherds were later released but the guerrillas kept the remaining three, including Grivas. There was much discussion over what to do with their prisoners. It was generally accepted that Grivas, who had been directly responsible for the death of Yerakakis, should die; but several believed the two others were innocent of wrongdoing and should be released. Some argued that as the three shepherds were members of the MAY they all deserved the death penalty. Eventually, the argument for killing the shepherds won the day and the three men were taken away and executed.

When the fate of the three abducted men became known, the shepherds in the foothill villages of the White Mountains were outraged. Recently all the shepherds had been compelled by the authorities to sign on as members of their local MAY: failure to do so meant that they would be refused permission to bear arms, and the shepherds needed a weapon to protect themselves and their flocks from sheep and goat thieves. The reality was that although all the shepherds had enlisted as members of the MAY, some of them had continued to give food and shelter to the guerrillas.

The deaths of the three shepherds and the loss of the 700 goats and the cheese-making equipment brought great hardship to their families. Taking advantage of the wave of unpopularity the guerrillas were experiencing, Colonel Vardoulakis led a large patrol to Anopolis, where he announced an amnesty for all army deserters and for those men who had not reported for duty on receiving their call-up papers. All who surrendered, Vardoulakis promised, would suffer no punishment and would be free to rejoin their units or, if they preferred, could enlist in the gendarmerie.

Many of the army deserters took advantage of this offer of amnesty and turned themselves in. Among those who surrendered was a young man who was in a unique position to do great damage to the communist movement in Canea.

George Tourlentes was a soldier from the mainland, who had been employed in clerical duties until the end of January, when he received instructions that he would be transferred to an infantry battalion. Before his transfer came through, Tourlentes visited some friends of an army colleague in a suburb of Canea. These friends were known left-wingers and Tourlentes told them of his reluctance to take part in infantry operations against the guerrillas. At the end of a long conversation, in which Tourlentes constantly expressed left-wing sympathies, he was invited to join the guerrilla army. He accepted the suggestion at once.

Instead of returning to his barracks that night, Tourlentes went into hiding in a nearby house. After four days he was moved to a different suburb. During the next month he was relocated on two more occasions before being taken one evening to a house just outside Mournies. A few nights later, he was collected by a guide and taken to Omalos where he joined up with Nikos Tsamantis and his band of guerrillas.

Tourlentes made no close friends among the guerrillas and many would later comment that he was often seen sitting alone, writing notes in his diary. He took part in the attack on the Lakki garrison and had afterwards sought refuge with the guerrillas in the Samaria Gorge. After escaping from the gorge, Tourlentes disappeared.

Two weeks later, thirty-six arrests were made in Canea and the authorities claimed that the whole of the clandestine network of the KKE in the town was in police custody. An announcement in the local press declared that the arrests had been made possible by an army deserter, George Tourlentes, who had surrendered and provided a detailed account of his time with the guerrillas. Tourlentes was able to name three of the people who had helped to recruit him and had given nicknames of others. The houses in which he had been hidden were identified and a close watch kept on them. Many of those named by Tourlentes were known to the authorities and some had been arrested previously. A few had even served short sentences in exile for communist activities and several others had been suspected of being a danger to public order but had not been arrested through lack of evidence. With the information supplied by Tourlentes and the results of their own surveillance the police moved swiftly one morning in synchronised raids throughout the town.

Among those arrested was Toula Tsitilos, who had assumed responsibility for the KKE organisation in the town when her husband took to the mountains a few months earlier. While her two-year-old daughter was being cared for by another woman, Tsitilos ran the KKE network so effectively that a steady supply of food, clothing, money and information made its way, with the occasional recruit, to the guerrillas in the mountains.

A vast collection of KKE literature and a radio were found in the house Tsitilos was using as a hiding-place. The printing press of the left-wing *Dimokratia* newspaper, which had been banned the previous year, was discovered in another house. For some time the paper had been published and distributed secretly within the town; all those involved it its circulation were arrested.

The thirty-six defendants, six of whom had been born in Asia Minor, were speedily brought to trial. Toula Tsitilos claimed that she had no political views but had been in hiding as she feared arrest and deportation because she was the wife of the KKE first secretary for the region of Crete. Mihali Biotakis, a former editor of *Dimokratia*, denied that he had organised the publishing of the newspaper and told the court that he had been lying low because, as a well-known left-winger, he was afraid of being murdered out of hand. The man accused of being behind the distribution of the newspaper claimed that he was employed to take packages to a particular shop and he had no idea of the contents of the packages. However, many of those arrested, some of whom were as young as eighteen, confessed to working for a banned organisation.

At the end of a brief trial, Tsitilos and Biotakis were sentenced to life imprisonment. The majority of their co-defendants were given prison terms of seven to fifteen years; a few were released through lack of evidence.

Since the start of the civil war the KKE had found it relatively easy to enlist new members for their movement from the countryside but in town this had always been difficult. The information provided by Tourlentes had severely damaged the communist setup in town and put a stop to this method of recruitment altogether.

One person who escaped arrest during the roundup of the communist network in town was Vangelio Kladou, who had been using a hide-out which was not known to Tourlentes. With most of her comrades betrayed and in custody, Kladou secretly left Canea and joined the guerrillas in the mountains.

During the trial Tourlentes had enraged the guerrillas with his public statements that morale among the guerrillas was very low and many were considering surrender. He insisted that the guerrilla forces had become ineffective due to the persistent army and gendarme patrols in the mountains and that victory over the guerrillas was in sight.

Tourlentes' prediction, that many of the guerrillas were on the verge of surrender, turned out to be true. Over the coming month there was a steady flow of guerrillas surrendering with their weapons and publishing their declarations of repentance in the local paper. Colonel Vardoulakis kept up the pressure on the guerrillas by increasing the number of patrols in the countryside. These efforts were rewarded when a guerrilla was taken by surprise and killed in a ruined house in Vamvakopoulo one afternoon. Within days, another guerrilla was killed at Marediana and two more were killed by a patrol in Palea Roumata. The patrol also made ten arrests and, as soon as it had left the village, locals burnt down five houses belonging to families related to guerrillas.

Written declarations of loyalty to the government were made from villages as far apart as Koxare in the east to Sirikari in the west and Agia Roumeli in the south, with all adult male villagers adding their signatures to the document. Official figures published for 18 April – 18 May 1948 claimed that 13 guerrillas had been killed, 10 captured and 46 had surrendered. Over the same period one gendarme had been killed.

By the end of May, pressure from the constant search parties had driven many guerrillas deep into the mountains. Patrols arrived in villages daily, rounding up suspected guerrilla supporters and burning houses that belonged to guerrillas. Gradually, the majority of the guerrillas sought refuge in the Samaria Gorge, where their camp had been re-established just to the north of the village of Samaria.

Colonel Vardoulakis now sought to bottle up the guerrillas in the gorge. Government troops occupied all the mountain paths out of the gorge and gendarmes landed by boat from Paleohora to complete the encirclement in the south.

As the guerrillas became aware that there was no longer any possibility of escape from the gorge, a few talked among themselves of surrender. One of the most outspoken guerrillas was Leonidas Kostourakis, who had served with the guerrillas since the beginning of the rebellion. He was well-respected by his comrades but his suggestion that they lay down their arms rather than fight a lost battle brought him into direct conflict with the leadership.

Kostourakis was brought before a Guerrilla Court. Officially, he was charged with keeping a gold sovereign that he had found in the tunic of the Lakki garrison commander, Lt Patsidiotis, who had been captured and executed a couple of months earlier. All the guerrillas,

The Eagles of Crete

however, understood that the real reason Kostourakis faced a Guerrilla Court was to make an example of him. After a brief trial, the veteran guerrilla was sentenced to death and executed.

A series of speeches was given by the guerrilla leaders to their men to raise their spirits. Unable to break out of the gorge, the guerrillas would be forced to fight but the *kapetans* insisted the gorge was impregnable. Although many of the men had eaten no bread for two months, there was no food shortage as there were still several hundred stolen sheep and goats in the gorge, as well as a good supply of yoghurt and cheese. There were few paths into their stronghold and many places where ambushes could be set. Heavy machine-guns were already in position at strategic points and the *kapetans* were confident that if the men remained resolute the gorge would be held. When the speeches were over, the guerrillas had a meal and then, until after midnight, heartened themselves with singing.

Colonel Vardoulakis had assembled around 1,000 men in the area of the gorge, determined to bring an end to the rebellion. Careful planning had gone into this offensive, based on information received from guerrillas who had been captured and those who had surrendered. All the guerrilla leaders were believed to be in the gorge with almost the entire guerrilla army and all known exits had been sealed. There would be no repeat of the failure experienced during the previous raid on the guerrilla base when the guards at Poria had relaxed their watch and allowed the guerrillas to escape. In addition to closing all paths, Vardoulakis had ordered that men with binoculars be posted on many of the mountain peaks to observe both sides of the gorge. Three doctors were with the government forces to tend the casualties in what was anticipated to be a major and decisive battle.

To defend the gorge, fifteen guerrillas were sent to guard the narrow route in from the south. Two dozen men took up position to guard the route to Samaria from Agios Ioannis in the southeast. Another twenty men hid among the pine trees below a steep and dangerous way into the gorge from Psari in the north-east. The rest of the guerrilla force moved northwards to defend the routes in from the Omalos Plateau and Poria.

For three days there was fighting as government troops attempted to enter the gorge from all directions. Eventually, the breakthrough came when gendarmes made a daring daylight assault on a strong guerrilla position defended by a heavy machine gun. The machine gunner was killed and two guerrillas were captured. Troops could hear the guerrillas shouting to each other as they began to withdraw from their advanced positions and fell back, deeper into the gorge. At a narrow part of the gorge near to Agios Nikolaos Church, eight guerrillas were left as a rearguard.

Early on the morning of the fourth day, the guerrillas guarding the Agios Ioannis path from the southeast retreated, leaving the way into the gorge open. Later that day, the men defending the route from Psari, to the northeast of the guerrilla camp, were forced back. As the guerrillas defending this route hid among the trees and giant boulders, troops moved down towards Samaria village.

When the troops reached the guerrilla camp they met fierce resistance, which was finally broken when *Kapetan* Panos was fatally shot in the spine. Originally from Edessa, Panos was one of the army deserters from Agios Nikolaos who had joined Podias and later made his way to the White Mountains. His feet wrapped in rags, Panos had rallied his men and held up the enemy advance for some time. Several of the men with him were shot dead and government forces took control of the camp and Samaria village.

Resistance at Agios Nikolaos church collapsed late that afternoon. Six of the guerrillas were killed and their leader, Nikos Xeroyannakis, chose to shoot himself with his own pistol rather than surrender. Among the dead were two of the aircraftsmen who had joined the communists after the seizure of Maleme airfield and two brothers from Voutas.

The gorge had fallen and the main body of guerrillas took up positions at Prinias, a thickly wooded area on the western side of the gorge. As gendarmes approached Prinias, two more guerrillas were killed in heavy fighting, which lasted until the evening.

Government forces now had control of all known escape routes from the gorge, as well as the guerrilla camp and abandoned guerrilla possessions. Many of the guerrillas at Prinias had no food or water and were short of ammunition. Several had long since worn out their boots and had fashioned footwear out of goatskins or rags, held together by wire and string. Their situation seemed hopeless.

As night was falling, Yanni Viglis, a shepherd from Samaria and brother of an ELAS hero who had been murdered by the MAY from Lakki a few months earlier, informed the guerrilla leaders that there was a way out of the gorge that started from Prinias and was known only to a few local shepherds. There was every expectation that this exit from the gorge, just beneath the summit of Volakias, would be left undefended.

The guerrillas gathered together and received their instructions. They were told the going was so rough and difficult that it was vital for each guerrilla to keep the person behind them in sight. One wrong step could be fatal but the precipitous route was their only hope of escape. Ninety guerrillas set off behind Viglis as he led the way up a small goat path.

Soon the goat path disappeared and the guerrillas were struggling up steep mountainside. They crossed bare rock, zigzagged between massive boulders, often using their hands to pull themselves up, with a sheer drop below them. Viglis showed no hesitation over the route.

The climb took several hours and there was only one casualty. Stavros Hatzigrigoris, the myopic lawyer, had trouble keeping up and slid several metres down the mountainside. No bones were broken but Hatzigrigoris moved even more slowly after his fall.

Just before sunrise the guerrillas emerged from the gorge. They made for some nearby cypress trees and when the sun came up were all well hidden. For the whole of that day they remained concealed from any spotter plane that might come over. The area they were in was surrounded by gullies and they sat around in small groups, saving their energy for the following night's march. Some of them drank their own urine in an attempt to slake their thirst. Viglis assured them they would find water the following night.

The day passed slowly. No planes flew over looking for them and as soon as it grew dark they once again fell in behind Viglis. For several hours they followed him southwards to a dried-up streambed.

Eventually, Viglis came to a halt beside some boulders. The guerrillas crowded round as he removed a large flat stone that covered a hole, at the bottom of which was a pool of stagnant water. There was only room for three at a time at the opening and, despite the poor quality of the water, the guerrillas drank their fill.

Later that day the guerrillas held a meeting and agreed that they should split into two groups. The larger group was to head west towards Koustogerako, thence north towards Prasses. Near Prasses this group would split up into smaller groups of six to fifteen and make their way back to villages where they were confident they could hide and obtain food. On the early part of this long route through the mountains there was only one known spring, near Pikilassos, and it was thought unlikely that government forces would be guarding it. A smaller group of a dozen, which included most of the leaders, was to go east and make for the villages of Sfakia.

When night fell, the two groups parted company. The group going west walked all night along the wild coast to Pikilassos. Here they found, as expected, that the spring was unguarded. They continued into the mountains high above Koustogerako and hid for the rest of the day. As soon as it grew dark, two guerrillas went down to the village and returned with rusks, cheese and several litres of olive oil.

Later that night they moved on again. When they were nearer to Prasses, they came across some shepherds who provided them with a plentiful supply of milk and cheese. Many of the guerrillas' stomachs were unable to cope with food after days of near starvation and they were sick, some of them for several days. As they recovered their strength they split up and moved off in different directions, to villages they were confident would feed them.

The smaller group making for Sfakia included *Kapetan* Mihali, George Tsitilos, and Yanni Manousakas. They were led by George Manousellis, a former Athens policeman from Kallikratis, but their progress was slow as the injured Hatzigrigoris found the going difficult. In silence they descended to the sea and made for the stream below Agia Roumeli. After drinking their fill of the clear mountain water they continued along the beach.

The Eagles of Crete

Before long they turned once more for the mountains and began a long climb up a steep gorge, reaching the top as the sun rose. Fortunately there was a heavy mist for most of that morning which concealed them from view so they continued walking until noon. A hiding-place was found and, after posting a lookout, the guerrillas settled down for some sleep. That night, as soon as it grew dark, they moved down to Agios Ioannis to obtain food and information.

The government forces, meanwhile, had spent a restless night awaiting the final battle with the guerrillas. Trapped in a small part of the gorge, the guerrillas were expected to put up a fierce, final resistance. When morning broke, the gendarmes, soldiers and the MAY advanced cautiously towards Prinias, imagining guerrillas hiding behind every boulder. One guerrilla, wounded in the leg and unable to move, was shot by the member of MAY who found him. Two other guerrillas, discovered in a hiding place, were surrounded and shot. But the main force of guerrillas was nowhere to be found.

The site of the guerrilla camp was examined carefully and all personal belongings left behind by the guerrillas and around 1,000 goatskins were collected up and burnt. In one place in the gorge 200 goats were found with their throats cut; in another, 250 sheep and goats were found alive. Among the weapons that were captured were a mortar and two heavy machine guns.

The following day, most of the government forces marched south to the sea near Agia Roumeli and were taken by warship to Paleohora. Some soldiers and gendarmes remained in the gorge with orders to continue the search for any guerrillas who had become separated from the main body and were in hiding. These search parties remained on patrol in the gorge for three more days without finding any further sign of life.

On 7 June 1948, Colonel Vardoulakis announced that fifteen guerrillas had been killed in the successful four-day operation in the Samaria Gorge and, from the quantities of blood found, several more were believed to be fatally wounded. On the government side, three gendarmes had been killed and five gendarmes and four members of the MAY wounded.

Vardoulakis confirmed that no respite would be given to the guerrillas and that operations against them would continue. He declared the offensive against the guerrilla stronghold to have been a great victory and forecast that the guerrillas who had escaped into the mountains would be forced to surrender, or would die of thirst or starvation.

Chapter 9
The Guerrilla Force Disintegrates

Spiro Fitrakis made a successful getaway as the order for retreat was given to the small band that had fiercely defended the path into the Samaria Gorge near Agios Nikolaos; all his comrades were killed. He was unable, though, to reach the main body of guerrillas at Prinias so he found a secluded place to hide. Thirty-seven-year-old Fitrakis, an ELAS veteran from Palea Roumata, would use all his cunning to avoid capture over the coming days.

As soon as darkness fell, he crawled towards a spring, constantly stopping to listen for sounds of movement. When the spring came into view he remained motionless, hidden behind a tree trunk. After keeping watch for some time to make sure he was not walking into an ambush, he approached without a sound and gulped down all the water his stomach could hold.

Before dawn came, Fitrakis made for some huge boulders beneath a precipice and found somewhere to hide. For the rest of the day he kept his eye on the spring in the hope that other guerrillas might show up. To his great disappointment the only sounds he heard were of a large force of gendarmes making their way through the gorge.

The following night he moved further into the gorge. Before he had gone far, he came across an enormous pine tree that had fallen across the streambed. Winter rains had washed away some of the soil beneath its trunk making a hole, almost large enough to hide him completely. Fitrakis set about enlarging the hole and carefully placed several large rocks in front of the pine before crawling into his new hide-out. He had little room to move but was completely hidden from view. For the rest of that day he stayed put, safe from the gendarmes whose yells, as they searched for hidden guerrillas, reached him now and then. Later in the afternoon all went quiet.

Fitrakis began to hope that the gendarmes had left the gorge and decided that his best chance of meeting up with his comrades again was to make for Samaria village and ask for news there. Avoiding the path, he took a more difficult and longer route through the undergrowth and on the way came across sage growing in abundance. He picked some and ate it. Having stuffed his pockets full of sage, he continued on his way.

As soon as Samaria came into view, he found a hiding place behind a tree some distance away and kept a careful watch to establish whether or not gendarmes were occupying the village. After a three-hour vigil his worst fears were confirmed when he spotted an armed patrol entering Samaria.

Fitrakis now realised that his only hope of safety and finding food lay in getting out of the gorge. He made his way to the east and began a steep climb up a goat path. It had been three months since he had been on this route out of the gorge and he prayed he would find his way in the darkness. Exhausted through lack of food, Fitrakis decided to lighten his load by hiding his weapons and ammunition. He made careful note of the hiding-place, confident that he would return one day to collect them.

The climb up the mountain path took him all night. As Fitrakis neared the exit from the gorge he moved even more slowly and carefully, afraid that gendarmes would be waiting in ambush. When he had ascertained as best he could that there were no gendarmes around he hastened to a nearby cheese-hut. There was no food in the hut but Fitrakis helped himself to a shepherd's crook that had been left there. Armed with this, he believed he could pass himself off as a shepherd if spotted at a distance by a patrol in the mountains.

Fitrakis headed north at a brisk pace in the cold early morning breeze. He covered a good distance, then headed west and found that he was in a steep gorge, descending rapidly. With some difficulty he negotiated a route and was overjoyed to chance upon a spring. He found a hiding place nearby and rested until it grew dark.

The Eagles of Crete

Fitrakis knew he must be near to Zourva and as soon as dusk fell he set off again. He was now on a better path and had not gone far before he thought he could make out some houses in the distance. A short time later he heard some dogs barking. Taking cover behind some carob trees, he rested until dawn.

Soon after the sun came up, the villagers started to go about their daily labours. Fitrakis kept watch and after several hours' observation decided there were no government forces in the area. Around the middle of the morning he made his way towards Zourva. At a spring he came across a woman leading a goat and was able to get confirmation from her that there were no gendarmes in the village. She also told him that Christos Boloudakis and half a dozen guerrillas were hiding nearby.

Fitrakis climbed up to Zourva and went to the *kapheneion* where he learnt that most of the guerrillas had escaped from the gorge to fight another day. A local then took him down a path to where Boloudakis and his men were hiding. They shared their food with him and told him they intended to remain in hiding near Zourva for a few days as the frequent army patrols made it difficult for them to move around.

Fitrakis was anxious to move on and a few days later left his comrades. Resting by day and moving at night it took him three days to reach an area near his village, which he knew well from pre-war hunting expeditions. He stopped at a stream and washed and then sheltered from the heat among some plane trees.

That night he went to the home of a cousin who had a house on the edge of Palea Roumata. The cousin was astonished to see him, having heard rumours that Fitrakis had been shot in the battle in the gorge and had crawled away to a hiding-place where he later died of his wounds. Fitrakis learnt that the luck he had enjoyed in the gorge had remained with him that night. He had just missed a gendarme patrol that had been in the village for several hours searching homes and questioning the occupants.

Later that day Fitrakis' brother, Stelios, informed of his whereabouts by the cousin, arrived with a meal of broad beans, bread and olive oil. Stelios brought bad news. A gendarme had approached him the previous day and informed him that the authorities knew his brother was alive and in or near Palea Roumata. Confirmation of his brother's escape from the gorge had come from one of the guerrillas he had recently met who had surrendered. The brothers discussed their course of action and concluded that Fitrakis had no alternative but to surrender.

In the middle of July, five weeks after his escape from the Samaria Gorge, Spiro Fitrakis surrendered to the nearest gendarme post. He was taken to Firka Fortress and held there for a month with several other guerrillas. The number of those being held increased with each passing day and when the cells became overcrowded the prisoners were taken to Souda and shipped to Piraeus. After a short journey by road to Lavrion they were put on a boat to the island prison of Makronisos.

The small band of guerrillas charged with holding the path from Psari, in the northeast of the Samaria Gorge, had also successfully escaped detection. When the troops withdrew from the summits, the guerrillas headed north out of the gorge and then split into smaller groups.

On 9 June, an army patrol spotted some armed men near the Tromarissa spring and fired on them. The guerrillas at first stood their ground and returned fire but after a few minutes fled the scene. On searching the area, the soldiers found some abandoned knapsacks and traces of blood. Later, when a more thorough search was made, a body was discovered in a nearby cave. A few hand grenades, a rifle, a large supply of ammunition, several pieces of clothing and some documents were found with the corpse.

A few days later seven guerrillas surrendered. Among those who gave themselves up were two of the aircraftsmen who had deserted from Maleme, including *Kapetan* Youras, the ringleader behind the capture of the airfield.

The following week, three more guerrillas were cornered near Milones early one morning by a gendarme patrol. They were called upon to surrender but refused to do so and the three men, armed with a machine gun, a rifle and a pistol, died fighting. Two of the dead guerrillas were Cretans but the third was identified as Tavronitis, the national serviceman from mainland Greece who had gone over to the guerrillas after the battle at Tavronitis in April 1947.

On 19 June 1948, a small band of guerrillas was surprised by a patrol of gendarmes who were lying in wait on a path near a farm in the hills above Fournes. The half dozen guerrillas fired off a few shots and fled. All escaped except for one severely wounded guerrilla who was captured and taken to hospital, where his leg was amputated. The following day the rest of the band surrendered at the gendarme post at Alikianos.

At the end of June, the authorities were able to chalk up further successes with the capture of Dionysius Mandakas and Eftichis Makrinakis. The two men were surrounded near Prasses, and after a brief gun battle, in which a gendarme was wounded, threw down their weapons and put up their hands. Both men had served in ELAS as *kapetans* and were highly respected members of the guerrilla army.

In the same month, several other guerrillas were killed as they made their way through the mountains alone. One, a guerrilla from the mainland who was wanted for crimes committed in the fighting in Athens in December 1944, was spotted hiding in a wooded area in a gorge just outside Sassalos. He was surrounded and ordered to surrender but was killed when he opened fire. Another guerrilla was shot and killed near Deliana after he was spotted by a gendarme patrol and made a run for it when called upon to surrender. A third was shot and killed when he tried to escape after being cornered by gendarmes in the mountains near Gournes.

The military court in Canea was soon busy dealing with the unrepentant members of the guerrilla army. George Papayannakis and Dimitri Ledakis, who had been captured hiding in Perivolia in April 1948, were among the first to be tried. Both men were found guilty of armed rebellion against the state, sentenced to death and shot by firing squad on 6 July. Later that month, Ledakis' sister Maria, who had been in the mountains with him, surrendered to the authorities.

At the trial of Dionysius Mandakas and Eftichis Makrinakis, eyewitnesses were produced who gave evidence that Mandakas had been present at the attack on Lakki the previous December. Two villagers testified that they had seen Mandakas during the night raid on their village and formed the impression that he was one of those in charge of the guerrillas. Another eyewitness confirmed that Makrinakis had taken part in the raid on Epanohori. Several other witnesses gave evidence that Mandakas and Makrinakis had joined up with Yanni Bandourakis from the beginning of the civil war and were both well known communists.

In his defence, 66-year-old Mandakas - the oldest member of the guerrilla army - admitted that it was true that he had been a communist in his youth but claimed he had abandoned communism later in life. He denied the accusations against him and maintained that he had been searching for some lost sheep on the day of his arrest. For his part, Makrinakis said that he had been helping Mandakas in his search for his sheep and had heard that guerrillas were in the area. When challenged by armed men he had opened fire, shooting and wounding a gendarme in the belief that he was shooting at guerrillas.

The trial lasted two days, and after adjourning for an hour to discuss the verdict, the president of the court sentenced both men to death. They were executed by firing squad a few days later.

Many of the guerrillas saw the hopelessness of their situation and turned themselves in to the authorities. The most senior guerrilla to surrender was Nikos Tsamantis, whose relatives, at his prompting, had spent ten days negotiating terms with the local military commander. Tsamantis surrendered with his younger brother, Dimitri, on 13 July. The following day their father was released from prison.

While the authorities celebrated, the surrender of Tsamantis was viewed with great concern by the guerrilla leadership. In an attempt to discourage other guerrillas from following his example, they issued a proclamation accusing Tsamantis of betraying a number of his comrades while negotiating to save his own skin. Traitors like Tsamantis, they warned, would swiftly receive their just punishment.

A few days later, Tsamantis made use of the local press to reply to these accusations in a letter addressed to the "People of Canea".

Tsamantis declared that many in Canea were familiar with his exploits in the dark days of the German occupation, especially those who lived in the mountain villages, and were in a perfect position to judge him. He had, he said, fought the Germans out of patriotism, had been wounded and suffered much hardship in his desire to liberate his country. He had joined the communist rebellion because he had believed the struggle was concerned with democracy and freedom but was depressed at the sorry state of affairs that had been reached. He was now convinced that Greek blood was being spilled to no purpose and he had surrendered in the hope that he could contribute to peace and security in his country.

Despite the threats of retribution from the guerrillas still at large, the steady stream of guerrillas who gave themselves up continued over the coming weeks. Among those who turned themselves in was Stelios Fitourakis, the soldier who had helped the guerrillas with the information leading to the capture of the Lakki garrison earlier that year. Lieutenant Patsidiotis, the garrison commander, had been listed as missing since his abduction by the guerrillas. Eyewitness accounts of Patsidiotis' execution were now plentiful and an army patrol was sent to the Xyloskalo entrance to the Samaria Gorge with precise instructions on the exact location to be searched. After combing the area for a short time, the commander's head and body were recovered, two hundred metres apart, at the bottom of the gorge. His remains were collected and taken to his family for burial.

On the day that Lt Patsidiotis' body was discovered, a reward of twenty million drachmas was announced for the capture, dead or alive, of *Kapetan* George and Fotis Anagnostakis.

Anagnostakis, a former member of ELAS, had murdered his uncle, a retired gendarme sergeant-major, the previous winter. Despite their political differences and the fact that he was a wanted man, Anagnostakis had often eaten at his uncle's home, safe in the knowledge that family ties would prevent his host turning him in to the authorities. At the end of January he had arrived at his uncle's home with some comrades and, as usual, had joined the retired gendarme for a meal. When they had finished eating, Anagnostakis invited his uncle outside for a private chat. His uncle left the house with him but as soon as he was outside the door, Anagnostakis shot him in the head.

A month after the discovery of Lt Patsidiotis' body, an army patrol finally caught up with Anagnostakis and trapped him with two comrades in the mountains above Meskla. After a brief battle, Anagnostakis' body was found alongside that of another of the guerrillas, but the third, a former aircraftsman from Maleme, despite being seriously wounded, managed to escape. The following morning the patrol made a thorough search of the area and found the man hiding in a small wood. To force him out of his hiding place the soldiers set fire to the wood but the wounded guerrilla remained where he was and was burnt to death.

To encourage the remaining guerrillas to give themselves up, Colonel Vardoulakis announced that those who did surrender and who were not wanted for committing any specific criminal acts could be released from custody after serving a short sentence. Official figures for the period 20 April to 4 August 1948 record that 37 guerrillas were killed, 14 captured and 174 surrendered.

Several of the guerrillas still on the run were coming under increasing pressure to surrender from members of their own families. One night, Christos Boloudakis received a message from his father and godfather to visit them in his native village of Meskla. Yanni Perakis, a long-serving guerrilla and close friend, accompanied Boloudakis to the meeting.

Boloudakis' father, egged on by his godfather, begged his son to surrender. Christos Boloudakis became angry and is said to have pulled out his pistol to threaten his godfather. His father intervened and there was a fight, at the end of which both father and godfather lay dead.

The local press seized on the story. For the first time in Cretan history a son had killed his father over political differences and the communist leaders were blamed for brainwashing the island's youth to such an extent that they were unable to distinguish between right and wrong. The double murder did great damage to the guerrilla cause. Guerrillas in hiding everywhere were asked by those helping them to explain how the son, a leading *kapetan* with the guerrillas, could commit such a monstrous crime.

The Eagles of Crete

The guerrillas who remained in the mountains in the months following their defeat in the Samaria Gorge were finding it increasingly difficult to survive. Gendarme patrols regularly set ambushes near to springs and searched many of the caves that had been used as hide-outs by ELAS. To avoid possible ambush sites, the guerrillas were forced to avoid main paths and walk over very rough ground. Often, local villagers were enlisted to assist the search parties and sometimes sent into caves the gendarmes were afraid of entering. Patrols would fire shots into thickly wooded areas and, occasionally, set them alight. Homes of well-known supporters and relatives of the guerrillas were surrounded by gendarmes at night and searched without warning.

The result of all this activity was that few villagers were willing to provide food and shelter to the guerrillas. This was usually out of fear that, if captured, the guerrillas might betray them. Guerrillas could only approach villagers known to them for help. Among the villagers there was a fear that a gendarme would dress in rags and pretend to be a guerrilla, only to return later and arrest them if they gave him anything to eat.

Many of the guerrillas were reduced to spending their nights scavenging cultivated areas for food. Potatoes were eaten raw as they could not risk a fire to cook them and unripe fruit and vegetables they came across often made them ill. At least the guerrillas were safe in the knowledge that the following day the farmers would be unable to report the loss of their stolen produce to the authorities for fear that they would be accused of voluntarily providing food to the guerrillas.

Frequently the doors of former supporters were barred to them, despite repeated requests from the guerrillas that a slice of bread be thrown out to them. Now and then a small number of guerrillas would go to a remote house or small hamlet at night and demand food. Often the villagers were short of food themselves, especially if they had children, and the guerrillas were never able to fill their bellies. Clothes were also difficult to come by. Villagers were unwilling to give clothing to the guerrillas in case the guerrilla was captured or surrendered and the clothing was recognised and traced back to them.

In desperation, a dozen starving guerrillas burst into the monastery of Agia Triada at Perivolia, just outside Canea. Most of them were dressed in filthy rags but a few, the better dressed, were in stolen army uniforms. With rifles at the ready they entered the church, where the abbot was conducting a service. They forced the abbot at gunpoint to take them to his office where they seized the monastery funds, amounting to two million drachmas. Hurriedly they snatched all the food they could find and disappeared back into the mountains.

It seemed that the guerrillas were a spent force. Encouraged by the frequent statements by the authorities that the few remaining guerrillas would surrender or be wiped out in the near future, villagers began to return to the Omalos. As shepherds grazed their flocks on the hillsides, farmers were once again able to plant potatoes on the plateau.

It was a month before the guerrillas turned up. As it grew dark, thirty armed men suddenly appeared at the shepherds' huts. The guerrillas were roughly shod and dressed in rags – confirmation, the authorities were quick to point out, that they were no longer being looked after by the villagers or supplied by any supporters in the town. The men were led by Christos Boloudakis and the shepherds were forced to hand over all the food they had with them.

The armed band was not seen again until one night in the middle of October when it suddenly materialised in Drakona. Lookouts were posted at the two main approach routes into the village while the rest of the guerrillas spent two hours going from house to house collecting food by force. They left as quickly as they had arrived. The following morning a large patrol of gendarmes arrived in Drakona and set off in pursuit.

For three days the patrol searched for the guerrillas without success. In the afternoon of the fourth day a gendarme spotted some guerrillas in the distance. The gendarmes then lost contact with their quarry but continued to search the area carefully. Later that day the guerrillas, unaware they had been seen by the patrol that afternoon, arrived at the place they intended to spend the night. Just as the guerrillas finished their evening meal the gendarmes caught up with them once again. No lookout had been set, and the patrol split into two groups to launch a surprise attack on the guerrillas in the failing light.

As the first shots rang out, the guerrillas seized their weapons and returned fire. After fifteen minutes the guerrillas made a run for it, carrying a seriously wounded comrade with them. The man later died and was buried under a thick bush on a small plateau some distance away. Behind them the guerrillas abandoned fifteen bedrolls, twenty kilos of meat, several kilos of sugar, lentils, potatoes and beans as well as some clothing, twenty army water bottles and two rifles.

In a bid to clamp down on villagers who might be sympathetic to the communists, several new measures were announced. Travel between villages in the countryside was not allowed from the setting of the sun until 6 am. During these hours, villagers were not allowed to open their doors to anybody but the official authorities. Shepherds living in hill villages in the White Mountains were only allowed to take their flocks a distance of 2 km from their village. Those who contravened this order would be arrested and tried by military court. All animals belonging to shepherds who broke the curfew would be confiscated by the government. This restriction on the movement of flocks affected shepherds living in more than thirty hill villages. In addition, the MAY was to be slightly reformed. Villagers were to form their own Home Guard, whose main purpose would be to protect their villages from the guerrillas and prevent them from obtaining food locally.

Villages throughout the prefecture began to announce their compliance with this order. In Anopolis a new Home Guard of 85 men was established and the men of Agia Roumeli formed a Home Guard of 30 men. The villagers of Prasses announced that they were forming a Home Guard of 24 men and their leader was to be a reformed guerrilla who had surrendered to the authorities six months earlier.

The great majority of the guerrillas who surrendered did not do any serious harm to the guerrilla movement by betraying hide-outs or naming contacts used by those who remained in hiding. Many of them had been put under considerable pressure from their families and relatives to surrender - some had wives and children - and consequently, as they had kept their mouths shut, they were still held in some regard by their former comrades. Even those who signed and published a declaration of repentance could be forgiven. The few who remained on the run were well aware that those who surrendered had not changed their political views overnight but had been unable or unwilling to put up with the hardship, danger and constant hunger and thirst endured by the fugitives.

However, a few of the guerrillas who surrendered accompanied army patrols in their search of the mountains and were despised as traitors by their former comrades. These men were very useful to their new employers as they were willing to betray the hide-outs and meeting places the guerrillas had used in the past.

At the end of October, a gendarme patrol with one of these informers spent a fruitless four days in the mountains east of Omalos. The patrol had set ambushes without success at different locations each day and night. On the fourth night, four men were seen approaching as the gendarmes waited in their ambush positions at a spot in the mountains the guerrillas had previously used as a meeting-place.

The unsuspecting men were George Tsitilos and Dimitri Makridakis and their guides and bodyguards, Vassili Koutalonis and Yanni Perakis. As the four guerrillas came closer they spotted the figures of the gendarmes in the distance. At first, they were not concerned as this was where they were expecting to meet some of their comrades, including Nikos Kokovlis and his followers. Unknown to them, Kokovlis and his party were resting nearby, waiting for dawn before moving to the meeting place.

As they approached, Koutalonis shouted to the figures in the distance, asking if Antonis was there. The officer in charge of the gendarmes replied that he was. The four guerrillas continued their approach but, a short distance from the patrol, something must have made them suspicious as they suddenly turned and made a run for it. The soldiers chased the four guerrillas and exchanged fire with them for over an hour as they ran through ravines and across mountainsides.

Makridakis was the first to die. Some time later, a kilometre further on, the patrol cornered and killed Tsitilos. Both guides, who had remained faithfully by the sides of their comrades until their deaths, escaped. The body of George Tsitilos, first secretary for the KKE in Crete, was immediately identified. None of the soldiers recognised the second corpse, and it was the former guerrilla with them who identified it as that of 32-year-old Dimitri Makridakis, a veteran communist from Neo Horio.

The soldiers cut off the heads of Tsitilos and Makridakis and left the bodies where they lay. The patrol then carried the two heads through several villages, stopping to display them to the locals, before taking them to Canea. There the heads were set up on the Kladissos Bridge at the eastern entrance to the town, beside the gendarme post.

Sympathetic shepherds came across Tsitilos' corpse the day after he died and covered it with stones. Later, two guerrillas, Eleftherios Iliakis and Vassili Koutalonis, went in search of Makridakis' body and gave it a similar burial.

On 19 October 1948, two boys were collecting logs for winter fuel from a wood near Malaxa when they walked into seven armed men. The boys were taken hostage and spent the next four hours with the guerrillas, who passed the time chatting, shaving and sewing up their old clothes. In the afternoon, just before the bus from Canea to Gerolakkos was expected, the party moved nearer to the road and took up positions behind bushes. When the bus came into view the guerrillas stepped out into the road, guns at the ready, and brought it to a halt.

The fifteen passengers were told to disembark. After helping themselves to the passengers' belongings and all the cash they had, the guerrillas ordered the driver to pour petrol over his vehicle. The driver was also the owner of the bus and he pleaded with the men not to destroy his livelihood. His appeals fell on deaf ears and the bus roared into flames. To give his men sufficient time to make their getaway, the guerrilla leader told the driver and passengers to remain where they were and not move for fifteen minutes.

It was two months before the guerrillas struck again. On 22 December, fifteen guerrillas set an ambush for the Prasses bus. A former guerrilla who had surrendered, received an amnesty and taken a leading part in organising the Home Guard in Prasses, had gone to

Canea two days earlier. He was expected to be a passenger on the bus that day.

The afternoon bus from Canea to Prasses stopped in Skines to allow a few passengers to disembark. Soon after it left the village it began to ascend slowly into the hills. There were twenty-five passengers on board, six of whom were women. Two of the passengers were armed: one was a gendarme and the other was a member of the Prasses Home Guard, but he was not the former guerrilla for whom the ambush had been planned.

Thick bushes by the side of the road on a bend concealed the guerrillas, just a few metres from the road. As the bus approached the bend where the guerrillas were hiding, the driver began to apply the brakes. The guerrillas opened fire.

There was pandemonium in the bus. Several passengers were hit, either by bullets or flying glass, and many screamed out in terror. A hand grenade was tossed into the bus, which had come to an abrupt halt after the engine was machine-gunned from close range. When the shooting stopped, four passengers were found dead in their seats.

The guerrillas emerged from their hiding places and ordered the passengers from the bus. Both the gendarme and the member of the Home Guard had escaped serious injury in the attack and as soon as they got off the bus they made a run for it. The member of the Home Guard did not get far. He stumbled into a ditch, was surrounded by the guerrillas and killed. The gendarme was luckier and managed to make his getaway to the army post at Alikianos and raise the alarm.

All the guerrillas were filthy, dressed in rags and later described as looking like charcoal burners, one of the dirtiest occupations at that time. Several had beards and some were barefoot. As soon as the passengers disembarked the guerrillas set about taking their food, coats, footwear and money. According to newspaper reports, the guerrillas even took the footwear and clothing from the dead. In all, over a million drachmas were taken from the passengers. After seizing all that was of value to them, the guerrillas made for the mountains.

The Eagles of Crete

Shocked by attacks such as these, some villagers who had hitherto provided food to the guerrillas decided to inform against the very men they had previously helped.

One afternoon just before Christmas a small group of guerrillas in the hills above Loutro was betrayed to a gendarme patrol. All the guerrillas managed to escape, except Stavros Hatzigrigoris, the short-sighted lawyer. Two months earlier Hatzigrigoris had gone to a cistern in the high mountains during the night to drink and fill his water bottle. Throughout the day he, and nine other guerrillas with him, had kept the cistern under observation and were convinced that the area was deserted. However, as three of the guerrillas reached the cistern, shots rang out. Hatzigrigoris leapt for cover and crawled away. In his haste to escape he lost his glasses and had spent the last two months stumbling around the mountains.

Hatzigrigoris was surrounded by the patrol, and when called upon to surrender, opened fire. From his refuge behind some boulders, Hatzigrigoris held off the patrol for some time but was eventually killed when a gendarme crept close enough to throw a grenade into his hideout. His mother and sister were told of his death in their island prison camp on New Year's Eve.

But the guerrilla numbers were not only being reduced because guerrillas were giving themselves up, or being killed or captured. Just before the battle in Samaria Gorge, George Botounas, a long-serving communist activist, had died of tuberculosis. Another guerrilla, Spiro Hadabis, a young shepherd from Drakona, had begun to show symptoms of the same disease that autumn. A fellow villager of Hadabis', Vassili Koutalonis, took a sample of Hadabis' bloody sputum in a bottle to a relative in Stilos. The relative took the sample to a clinic in Canea for examination, explaining to the doctor that it was from an elderly relative in his village who was unable to come to the clinic himself. The sample was tested and the diagnosis of tuberculosis was confirmed.

Hadabis remained in hiding in damp caves in the mountains with his comrades, who looked after him as best they could, despite the risk of infection. It was winter, and Hadabis' health declined rapidly. Towards the end, in one of his more lucid moments, Hadabis made clear to the others that after his death he wanted his rifle to be passed to his sister Athina, who was in hiding elsewhere with another band of guerrillas.

Hadabis died one afternoon and was buried in a small, narrow cave in a remote part of the mountains. To ensure his body would not be found, the guerrillas stuffed branches into the cave's entrance and planted some bushes as a screen in front of it. With the entrance completely blocked, nobody passing that way would ever suspect the existence of the cave.

At the beginning of 1949, seven months after the battle in Samaria Gorge, there were just over forty guerrillas in the mountains of western Crete, eight of whom were women. There were seven others, all men, in hiding throughout the rest of Crete.

Only three members of the central committee of the Cretan KKE were still at large. Two of them, George Kontokotsos and Dr Emmanuel Siganos, were in the eastern part of the island; Vangelio Kladou was in Canea. Since their defeat in the Samaria Gorge, the guerrillas had been scattered in small groups, often with little or no contact between them. In an effort to re-establish the guerrillas as a force, Kladou sent a message to the older and more experienced Dr Siganos, requesting that he come to Canea and take control of the movement. Meanwhile, until Dr Siganos arrived, Kladou assumed the leadership of what was left of the guerrilla army and appointed Nikos Kokovlis as her second in command. Messengers were sent to all the guerrillas whose whereabouts were known with instructions to come to a meeting at the shepherds' huts at Hosses in the White Mountains at the beginning of April.

Dr Siganos had been hiding in Heraklion for over a year. As soon as he received Kladou's message he set off for Canea prefecture and with a network of helpers got as far as a small village near Episkopi. There he was hidden in a barn and told to await the arrival of Christos Boloudakis who was to take him the remaining part of the journey to the White Mountains.

Boloudakis arrived to collect Dr Siganos on 28 March but before he could do so was spotted by a member of the local Home Guard who knew he was a stranger in the area and thought he was acting suspiciously. The Home Guard was mobilised at once and Boloudakis made a run for it. A search of the area was made and Dr Siganos was discovered in his hiding-place and arrested.

While in Canea in prison awaiting interrogation, Dr Siganos attempted to commit suicide by cutting his wrists. His guards, on a routine visit to his cell, found him before he had lost too much blood, bandaged his wounds and saved his life.

The capture of Dr Siganos, a veteran communist with great influence and many contacts, was a severe loss to the KKE movement on the island and the authorities remained confident that the few fugitives still in hiding would soon surrender.

Chapter 10
The Net Tightens

Yanni Manousakas was among the 90 guerrillas who had escaped from the Samaria Gorge under the guidance of Yanni Viglis. When this group split up he joined the smaller party which headed east. After a few days, Manousakas left his companions and made for Rethymnon, in the hope of finding a boat to the mainland.

In Zouridi he made contact with an uncle and remained in hiding while inquiries were made about passage to Piraeus. For over a month Manousakas waited patiently. Eventually he was told that escape from Crete by boat was impossible as the police were checking the identities of all passengers and making thorough searches of all boats leaving the harbours.

Disappointed, Manousakas returned to the high mountains and for two months stayed with some shepherds who had sheltered him in the past. With the onset of bad weather, the shepherds were forced to take their flocks down to the hill villages for the winter and Manousakas descended to Kares on the Askifou plateau. A shepherd he knew there gave him a haircut and some clean clothes and late one night he set off through the Asfendos gorge to Vouvas, where he sought help from an ELAS veteran, Prokopis Boliotis.

As a long-term hide-out, Boliotis suggested a nearby cave at the bottom of the cliffs by the sea, one hour's walk from the village. The entrance to the cave was small and narrow but opened out into an enormous cavern. The main drawback was the constant noise of the waves breaking on the nearby rocks. For two months Manousakas hid in this cave, well-supplied with food and newspapers by Boliotis.

One night, Boliotis came to Manousakas and told him that he had received a message from George Manousellis, the leader of a number of guerrillas in hiding above Agios Ioannis. Manousellis had asked Boliotis to let him know of any guerrillas who had gone to ground in his area and to put him in contact with them. Towards the end of February 1949, after seven months of hiding alone, Manousakas left his cave one night and set off to meet Manousellis, who took him to his hide-out.

There were seven other guerrillas hiding with Manousellis among the pine and cypress forests in the mountains near Kato Kroussia. Among these were *Kapetan* Mihali, Manousakas' replacement as senior commander of the guerrilla army, and four female guerrillas. There was a big campfire at Manousellis' hide-out and security was lax. Manousellis and his party had been in the area for some time and their presence was known to the inhabitants of Agios Ioannis, who kept them supplied with food.

However, when two strangers were spotted near the camp in early March, the guerrillas decided it was time to move on. As the sun went down, they left Kato Kroussia and arrived at Kali Lakki, deserted by shepherds at that time of the year, just before dawn.

Kali Lakki was just above the snow line and the guerrillas were unable to light a fire lest they attract attention. For a week they stayed in Kali Lakki but, once again, when strangers were spotted in the area, the decision was made to move on, this time to shepherds' huts above Melidoni on the northern side of the White Mountains.

The eight set off that night. They moved off slowly, careful to avoid treading in the patches of snow and leaving their footprints for any patrols to find. For over a kilometre, they walked on rocks and stones and kept to the steep hillside where there was less snow. All night they headed north and at sunrise rested amongst some boulders that sheltered them from the wind. Patches of mist guaranteed their security. They ate the remains of the food they had with them and as soon as it began to get dark set off once again.

There was occasional ice under the snow on the northern side of the mountains and the guerrillas frequently slipped as they attempted to negotiate their way in the dark. In the end, they were forced to descend to avoid the ice, but their progress was slowed by the bitterly cold north wind. Just before dawn they arrived at a deserted shepherd's hut. Inside the hut the guerrillas lit a fire to warm themselves and dry their clothes. That night two of them went down to the nearest village to ask for food. They returned around midnight with a generous supply of bread, oil and beans and this was supplemented by some wild greens that were found growing near the hut.

Manousellis had been informed of the planned assembly of all the guerrillas at Hosses at the beginning of April, and as the day of the meeting approached he and his comrades moved off. Following the deaths of Tsitilos and Makridakis, the guerrillas were extra careful when they approached Hosses. To ensure the meeting had not been betrayed they arrived in the area the night before and kept careful watch for patrols. Before moving towards the rendezvous point itself, they imitated the clucking sound of a partridge to alert their comrades to their arrival.

In total, thirty-one guerrillas — twenty-five male and six female - were at the meeting. Messengers had been unable to make contact with the other guerrillas who were still on the run, all believed to be in hiding in Kissamos.

Five of the missing guerrillas were non-Cretans. *Kapetan* George, Athanasios Katsiferis and Stamatis Mariolis were from the Peloponnese; the other two, both army deserters from Agios Nikolaos, were Yanni Nikolopoulos, from Athens, and Manoli Frangiadakis, from Salonika. The two missing female guerrillas, Georgia Skevaki and Xenoula Athanasaki, were thought to have returned to Kissamos where they had many relatives to shelter them.

Athina Hadabi received her brother's rifle and much sympathy from all those present. Spiro Hadabis had been greatly respected by all who knew him and his loss was keenly felt. Many of the guerrillas had lost a family member in the civil war and almost all of them had at least one relative serving a sentence of exile in a remote prison camp.

Christos Boloudakis was full of remorse for the murder of his father and godfather but explained to his comrades that they had tried to force him to hand himself in to the authorities. The pair had earlier persuaded his youngest brother, Stavros, to surrender. Boloudakis was a popular *kapetan* but many of them listened to the story of the murders in horror. Not only did he face general disapproval over the killings but Boloudakis was also heavily criticised for failing to collect Dr

Siganos from his hiding place and was held partly responsible by many of the guerrillas for the doctor's capture.

The civil war was going badly for the communists on the mainland. In the winter of 1948-49, the aid the guerrilla army received from neighbouring communist regimes had been considerably reduced and, a few weeks before the guerrilla meeting in Crete, the government had declared the Peloponnese to be free of rebels. With the volume of U.S. aid on the increase, defeat for the communists seemed a certainty. Despite this, the thirty-one guerrillas at Hosses vowed to continue the struggle. Vangelio Kladou and Nikos Kokovlis were confirmed as the new leaders of the organisation.

Kladou gave her assembled comrades an account of the death of Dimitri Kontokonstantis. Kontokonstantis had taken part in the fighting in Athens in December 1944, following which he had been sentenced to death. With a price on his head, he had fled to Crete and sought refuge in the mountains. From 1946 he had been a trusted, reliable member of the guerrilla army. He knew several of the secret hide-outs and meeting places in the mountains as well as many of the dependable contacts in the villages who supplied food and information to the guerrillas. However, after the death of Tsitilos he had become depressed and argumentative and was suspicious of all his comrades. In fear for his life, he walked around with his pistol constantly cocked and was a danger to his companions. Convinced that he and the half dozen guerrillas he was hiding with were certain to be killed, he set off one night to walk to the nearest gendarme post to surrender. His fellow guerrillas had been keeping a close eye on their disturbed comrade and managed to catch up with him as he approached the nearest village. They seized him and took him back up into the hills.

The guerrillas were in no doubt that Kontokonstantis, with his detailed knowledge of the organisation, could not be allowed to surrender to the enemy. A discussion was held amongst the guerrillas present and the decision was made to execute him. The sentence was carried out that night.

At the Hosses meeting this execution was unanimously approved of by the guerrillas present. All agreed that no guerrilla could be

The Eagles of Crete

allowed to surrender if he was likely to cost the life of another guerrilla or cause severe damage to their movement.

The guerrillas, having agreed a time and place for their next meeting, split into groups and made off in different directions. Yanni Manousakas once again joined up with Manousellis, who led a group of ten back to Kato Kroussia, the hide-out above Agios Ioannis he had left a month earlier.

Soon after their arrival, Manousellis heard from a local shepherd that there were three large patrols of gendarmes in the area. At present they were limiting their movements to the foothills and along the coast, but it was only a matter of time before they came higher into the mountains. The guerrillas decided to move on, and headed east, keeping high in the mountains, and making for Kallikratis. That evening, as soon as darkness fell, Manousakas and another guerrilla, George Romanias, left the others and set off for Embrosneros.

Among those remaining with Manousellis was the veteran guerrilla George Miaoulis. Miaoulis had been born in Canea and was working in Ioannina when the Italians invaded Greece. A reservist officer, he was called up and saw action on the Albanian front. Unable to escape to Crete during the occupation, he remained on the mainland and later joined up with ELAS in Akarnania.

Other members of the party were Andreas Kourkoumelakis, a cobbler from Canea; an army deserter from Agios Nikolaos, known only by the pseudonym of Lycurgus; Sotiris Psarakis, a guerrilla from Kissamos; and George Christou, an Athenian. There were also two female guerrillas: Athina Hadabi and Eleni Papayannaki.

Manousellis was from Kallikratis and he was able to call on some of his relatives for help in sustaining his band. However, there was a shortage of communist supporters in the area and Manousellis was forced to trust anybody he could find. All went well for a few days but word soon spread that guerrillas were in hiding near Kallikratis.

On the morning of 18 April 1949, a young man delivered food and cigarettes to the cave at the usual time. As he left, members of the local Home Guard moved forward and surrounded the cave so quietly that the eight fugitives heard and suspected nothing.

Without warning, the Home Guard opened fire and in a matter of minutes six of the fugitives lay dead. Two, Andreas Kourkoumelakis and George Miaoulis, managed to make a run for it and were hotly pursued. Kourkoumelakis headed southwest a short distance and hid near Vouvas. Following a systematic search of the area he was soon found, surrounded in his hide-out, and shot when he refused to surrender.

George Miaoulis headed west and, two days later, took refuge with a shepherd who gave him food and shelter for the night. The following day the shepherd's brother betrayed Miaoulis to a patrol of the Home Guard from Hora Sfakion. On the way to Hora Sfakion for interrogation Miaoulis attempted to escape and was shot and killed.

A month later, two more guerrillas were taken by surprise and killed by a gendarme patrol while hiding in a small olive grove north of Kaina. Mathios Makridakis and Ilias Iliakis had taken cover in the grove earlier that morning. Both men were dressed in rags and had only a few stale crusts of bread in their knapsacks, but they were well armed and had a large supply of ammunition and several hand grenades. They believed they were well concealed behind a stone wall and soon became careless over their security.

That afternoon, a dozen gendarmes set off from Neo Horio on a routine patrol to Vamos. Their route took them via the olive grove where the two guerrillas were hiding. By chance, the patrol came upon the guerrillas from the rear and one of the gendarmes spotted the two armed men sitting in the field. The gendarmes quietly spread out to encircle them. Stonewalls in the area provided plenty of cover for the gendarmes and by the time the guerrillas caught sight of them they were surrounded. The sergeant in charge of the patrol called on the suspects to surrender but the two guerrillas responded by opening fire.

The shooting went on for half an hour; when it ceased the two guerrillas lay dead. One gendarme was wounded in the leg and died later on his way to hospital. The only item of interest found was a diary, discovered in Makridakis' pockets, which gave details of his recent movements and the operations in which he had taken part.

The Eagles of Crete

After their defeat in the Samaria Gorge the previous year the guerrilla leadership had threatened to execute any guerrilla who surrendered and betrayed them. One guerrilla who was considered a traitor by the communists had returned to live and work in Gavalohori, his native village. Late one night in early May, Spiro Blazakis, who was also from Gavalohori, took three men and hid just outside the village, close to the fields where their former comrade was expected to work the next morning.

Just after 8 am the former guerrilla and his father-in-law arrived for work. As soon as they had the two men in their sights, the guerrillas opened fire. The former guerrilla was killed outright and his father-in-law, who had no previous association with the guerrillas, was seriously wounded in the stomach. The firing attracted a number of villagers who were working nearby and Blazakis was recognised as he made his getaway. The father-in-law was rushed to hospital, where he was successfully operated on and made a complete recovery.

In the middle of July, a second assassination was planned of a former guerrilla, Constantine Foundoulakis, who was living in Kokkino Horio. Forty-five-year-old Foundoulakis had been born in Alikambos and had served with ELAS and the Democratic Army. When he became convinced that the defeat of the communists was inevitable he had accepted an amnesty from the authorities and resettled in Kokkino Horio. His attempt to start a new life had been successful but somebody in the village had tipped off the guerrillas that he would be visiting Plaka that day.

All through the heat of the afternoon, George Tzobanakis and Vassili Koutalonis lay in wait for their intended victim near the track between Plaka and Kokkino Horio. Eventually, at 8 pm, Foundoulakis came into view. He was alone. When he got to within a few metres of the two guerrillas, they opened fire, killing him instantly.

Unknown to Tzobanakis and Koutalonis, two large gendarme patrols had arrived in the area during the course of the afternoon, one at Plaka and the other at Kokkino Horio. The two patrols had begun a slow methodical search of the area between the two villages, making directly for the spot where Tzobanakis and Koutalonis were hiding.

Both search parties of gendarmes heard the gunfire and immediately set off towards it. Tzobanakis and Koutalonis emerged from their hiding place and made for Plaka. Almost immediately they spotted the gendarmes and turned and ran. As they fled towards Kokkino Horio, they discovered that gendarmes were also approaching from that direction.

The gendarmes opened fire and gave chase. For a short distance the guerrillas stayed together but then they split up, Koutalonis heading inland and Tzobanakis making for the sea. As they hastened after their quarry, the gendarmes spread out. Koutalonis was chased for two more hours before being cornered and killed by his pursuers.

George Tzobanakis made it to the sea unscathed. He was fortunate that along that stretch of coast there were many large boulders that hid him completely from view. As soon as he was certain that he was out of sight of the gendarmes he took off some of his equipment and hid it carefully. Tzobanakis was a good swimmer and by swimming and wading along the coast he reached a remote spot where he could hide and await for night to fall and aid his getaway.

The gendarmes chasing Tzobanakis sent for reinforcements as soon as they lost sight of him. Among those called upon to join the search were the twenty men of the Kokkino Horio Home Guard. A patrol boat arrived from Souda and sailed slowly along the coast; when darkness fell it directed its searchlights at the coastline. Despite all their efforts, the various search parties were unable to find Tzobanakis and they eventually called off the hunt for the night. Lookouts were left at strategic points to watch out for the lone guerrilla.

The search restarted early the following morning. Around noon, Tzobanakis' haversack, binoculars, rifle and ammunition belt were discovered carefully hidden behind a boulder by the sea. Inside the haversack were some grenades and a list of names of members of the Home Guard from nearby villages, presumed to be a list of possible future victims. Tzobanakis' trousers and boots were found beside the rest of his gear. There was no trace of Tzobanakis, who had successfully escaped during the night to a remote cave along the coast some distance away where Pagona Kokovli and Yanni Lionakis were hiding.

Exactly one month after Koutalonis' death another guerrilla was shot and killed in an ambush just outside Therisso. Yanni Perakis, a former member of EAM, went to the village with Argiro Baras, one of the deserters from the Agios Nikolaos garrison, in the hope of obtaining food. They were aware that search parties had recently been very active in the area. Only the previous week a gendarme had been killed when two patrols near Drakona had walked into each other at night and opened fire, each convinced they had come across a party of guerrillas. On the day that Baras and Perakis went to Therisso the military authorities had set several ambushes around the village.

Perakis and Baras approached the village cautiously but were spotted by some of the gendarmes lying in wait for them. The gendarmes shouted to the pair of armed men to halt and opened fire when Perakis and Baras turned and ran. Baras escaped unscathed but Perakis was shot in the head and killed instantly.

For some time a watch had been kept on certain houses and citizens in Canea. The previous year, following information from Tourlentes, the secret KKE network had been broken up but recently the police had received information that it was being re-formed.

Very early one morning they moved to round up all the suspects. Altogether, 48 arrests were made. The biggest catch was George Zografakis who was known to have been hiding in Canea for three years and was believed to be the new leader of the KKE committee in the town. He had been living in the old Jewish quarter and was asleep when the police arrived for him at 4 am. Alerted by the owner of the house, he climbed out of his bedroom window and, half naked, unsuccessfully attempted to escape over the neighbouring rooftops. Zografakis was taken to Canea police station where he was put in solitary confinement.

Ten days after his arrest, Zografakis was taken to Palea Roumata with a police escort. He had agreed to point out the places the guerrillas had used as hide-outs and cached weapons but soon after arriving in the village he made a run for it and was shot and killed.

A few days after the death of Zografakis, five men, aged between thirty-one and forty-five, all members of the KKE, were arrested in Palea Roumata. The five were found to be in possession of an assortment of weapons and ammunition as well as a radio that had been stolen from Maleme airfield. Some of them had taken part in the battle at Tavronitis at the beginning of the civil war and all confessed that they had hidden and fed guerrillas. Two of them had received an amnesty in September 1947 but had continued to assist the guerrilla movement.

The forty-seven arrested on suspicion of being members of an illegal organisation in Canea town were swiftly brought to trial. They were charged with having contact with and aiding armed bands that were planning acts of sabotage, robbery and arson with the aim of destroying the state. They were also accused of making collections of money and food with which to supply the guerrillas and of listening to the banned broadcasts made from the Greek Communist station in Eastern Europe and of passing news and propaganda to others. One of the forty-seven was charged with being the messenger between the organization in the town and the guerrillas in the countryside.

All the accused pleaded innocent and denounced the KKE but, after a two-week trial, thirty-four of the defendants were found guilty. Two were sentenced to death, three received life terms and another thirteen received prison sentences ranging from three to twenty years. Sixteen received lighter sentences and thirteen were released through lack of evidence.

The breaking up of the KKE organisation in the town was completed early one morning in September 1949 when a raid was carried out on a house in Vamvakopoulo. After a careful search, the communist printing press was discovered hidden in the cellar. The only entrance to the cellar was through a hole in the thin layer of concrete that formed the ceiling. A large earthen pot covered the entrance-hole when the cellar was not in use. Three boxes of printing type and a large supply of paper were found along with the press. Four arrests were made.

George Romanias and Yanni Manousakas had stayed with shepherds in the Embrosneros area for two months but, unable to agree on where

The Eagles of Crete

to go next, decided to part company and meet up again in the autumn. Manousakas returned to the mountains where he had shepherd friends he knew he could trust and Romanias set out for his native Kastellos, intending to collect some new clothes and footwear and spend the summer hiding near his village.

George Romanias, a former ELAS *kapetan*, had fled to the mountains in the summer of 1945 following a gun battle with a band of nationalists who had arrived at his family home in Kastellos to search for hidden weapons. After he escaped, his sister, Athina, was shot and killed as she attempted to hide a machine gun in a well.

Romanias had a cousin from Kastellos who was wanted for murder and was also hiding out locally. This cousin learnt that Romanias had returned to the area, was in contact once more with his family and was hiding in a small forest near the village. In the course of time the two men met up and would often share meals and spend time together.

The cousin is said to have made contact with Colonel Vardoulakis, the commander of the gendarmerie, and made an agreement with him. In return for killing Romanias the cousin was promised an amnesty, two hundred gold sovereigns, a passport and relocation to the U.S.A. Vardoulakis provided poison for the cousin to put in Romanias' food on the next occasion he met up with him.

The cousin did as instructed and added the poison to Romanias' meal, which he took to Romanias in his hideout. As soon as the poison had taken effect the cousin ran to inform the nearest gendarme post that Romanias was dead. Several gendarmes arrived on the scene and fired their rifles into the air to give the impression to anybody in the vicinity that a gunfight was taking place. They then took Romanias' body with them and paraded it through the villages from the back of a truck. In Souda they hung up the body in the square for public display. An official announcement was made that Romanias had been ambushed and killed by a gendarme patrol.

In the middle of October 1949, four guerrillas went down to the main Canea-Rethymnon road and hid near a small church between Vrisses and Agii Pandes. As soon as it grew dark, they dragged a large branch from a cypress tree into the road to set up a roadblock. There was little traffic, but after a brief wait a taxi came along from the direction of Canea. The driver drew to a halt as soon as he saw the cypress branch on the road ahead of him and the four armed men standing beside it with rifles pointed at his car.

The cab contained two passengers, wealthy livestock dealers who were on their way to Heraklion where they planned to buy some animals. The passengers and the driver were ordered out of the taxi and told to hand over their money and cigarettes. One of the livestock dealers was a leader of his local Home Guard unit and he recognised two of the guerrillas. He was later able to inform the authorities that the Iliakis cousins, Angelis and Eleftherios, were two of the four men who had carried out the ambush.

The guerrillas had just begun a careful search of the dealers' possessions when a jeep arrived from the opposite direction. Hurriedly the guerrillas took up position on both sides of the road and, after the jeep had come to a halt at the roadblock, shouted to the passengers to identify themselves. There were three men and two women in the jeep and the driver shouted back that they were the gendarmerie. Without warning, the guerrillas opened fire for a few seconds and then made a run for it.

Lieutenant Colonel Emmanuel Voutirakis had been making his return journey from Rethymnon to Canea when his jeep was stopped by the roadblock. With him in the jeep, besides the driver, were his wife, Helen, daughter Maria, and a nephew who was a sergeant in the gendarmerie. The driver and daughter were unharmed; the lieutenant colonel was wounded in one arm; and his nephew was hit several times in the body. The nephew was to die of his wounds the following day. Helen Voutiraki had been shot in the head and had died instantly.

The authorities promptly unleashed a wave of retribution on the relatives of the guerrillas and those suspected of helping them. Arrests were made throughout Apokoronas of over a hundred villagers who were related to the guerrillas or suspected of helping them. Some of those arrested were put in Canea prison and others were deported to Lasithi, where they were made to do agricultural work.

The Eagles of Crete

The day after the ambush of the jeep carrying Lieutenant Colonel Voutirakis and his family, the communist leadership on the mainland issued a proclamation through its radio station in Bulgaria stating that it was calling a cessation to hostilities. Following defeat in their last two mountain strongholds of Grammos and Vitsi in northern Greece, the guerrillas of the Democratic Army had withdrawn northwards to the neighbouring communist countries.

But the killing had not finished in Crete. On 22 November, Spiro Blazakis and George Tzobanakis took shelter in a remote spot between Kokkino Horio and Drapanos. Blazakis had served in Albania with the Cretan Division during the Italian invasion but had suffered frostbite in his feet and been sent back from the front. In the Battle of Crete he had fought at Agia and was a *kapetan* in ELAS. Blazakis had taken to the mountains after being sentenced to eleven years imprisonment in absentia in March 1947 for carrying a weapon. Tzobanakis had just been called up for military service when war broke out and fought the Germans at Heraklion. A native of Kokkino Horio, he had joined ELAS in the mountains in 1944. Fearing arrest for his political beliefs he had fled his village in the spring of 1947. The two men were intending to spend the day in their secluded hide-out and make for Drapanos that night to collect food from one of their supporters.

Stilianos Koundourakis was originally from Kissamos but had moved to Kokkino Horio with his wife and four children when he was offered employment as a lighthouse keeper. He was well-known for his nationalist views and, because he was right-wing, was readily granted a permit to own a hunting rifle. Early in the morning of 22 November he set off alone on a hunting trip to the remote area in which the two wanted men happened to be hiding.

The two guerrillas spotted the hunter as he approached their hide-out. Both of them prayed the man would change direction and not detect them. As he cast around for something to shoot, Koundourakis had no suspicion that he was walking directly into the hiding place of two of the most wanted men in Crete. The first he knew of the men's presence was when they shouted to him to drop his rifle. He did so immediately he saw two men a few metres away, pointing guns at him.

The guerrillas were faced with the dilemma of keeping Koundourakis with them until darkness and then releasing him as they made their escape from the area, or of killing him. They did not take long to make up their minds.

Later that day, a small search party of his friends went looking for Koundourakis after his wife informed them of his overlong absence. Afraid that he may have suffered a bad fall or an accident of some sort, his friends set off for the area to which his wife believed he had gone. After a careful search they eventually found their friend's body. Koundourakis had been shot in the chest and a note left with his corpse stated: "This is how enemies of the people are punished".

The final guerrilla attack of the civil war on a military target in Crete took place a couple of days later. Just before midnight, three guerrillas crept slowly and silently along the banks of the river towards the Kladissos Bridge, just outside Canea, where two gendarmes were on guard duty.

There was no movement on the road and the three guerrillas managed to crawl to within a few metres of the two gendarmes. They waited, listening carefully for any noise to break the silence. Satisfied that nobody else was around, the three guerrillas opened fire, fatally wounding the gendarmes. The guerrillas ran forward, grabbed the gendarmes' rifles, caps, tunics and boots and made their getaway into the darkness.

Chapter 11
The Perfect Hiding Place

A patrol made up of five gendarmes and four members of the Karkanis family began a search of the mountains above Hosses one morning in early December 1949. Members of the Karkanis family were with the gendarmes following the discovery in the mountains three months earlier of the body of their relative, 60-year-old George Karkanis.

On the same day the patrol set out, the two guerrilla leaders, Vangelio Kladou and Nikos Kokovlis, were making their way to a cave high in the mountains above Hosses. With them were three other guerrillas, including Dimitri Tsangarakis, a former senior activist with EPON.

The weather was bad, with heavy showers and mist settling over the mountains. When they arrived at their destination the guerrillas lit a fire so that they could dry their clothes and prepare a hot meal. In such bad weather and at such an altitude they agreed it was unlikely that there would be anybody in the high mountains at that time of year.

In the late afternoon the mist cleared briefly. Meanwhile the nine members of the patrol had arrived in the same area the guerrillas were in and one of the sharp-sighted gendarmes noticed a plume of smoke coming from amongst the large boulders in the distance. The patrol set off in the direction of the smoke.

At the cave the guerrillas began to prepare their meal. They had a large tin can that they used as a cooking pot and they filled this with water and put it on the fire. The meal that day was to be lentils and potatoes. Two of the guerrillas took firewood to the cave and as they set off to collect water from the nearest spring they spotted the gendarmes. The two guerrillas fired first and a battle broke out.

Kladou, who was sitting at the cave entrance beside the fire, was hit several times and killed before she could reach for her weapon. Tsangarakis was hit in the stomach and lay groaning in pain for some time before falling silent. For almost five hours the two sides exchanged fire but as darkness fell the guerrillas used the cover provided by the boulders to slip away into the night.

When no more shots came from the guerrillas, the patrol cautiously approached the cave. At its entrance they found the bodies of Tsangarakis and Kladou, who was clad in a soldier's uniform and army boots several sizes too big for her. Inside the cave were five greatcoats and two knapsacks, one containing documents, including Kladou's diary.

The heads of the two dead guerrillas were hacked off and carried back to Canea where they were impaled on spikes at the Kladissos Bridge. The population of the town hurried from their homes and large crowds gathered to view the gruesome sight. After a couple of days, the heads were thrown into the river.

In the same week that Tsangarakis and Kladou were killed, *Kapetan* George was betrayed and cornered. The authorities in Kissamos received a tip off that *Kapetan* George would be visiting a house in Rogdia that night and, early in the afternoon, parties of gendarmes set up carefully concealed ambushes on all approaches to the village. Towards seven o'clock that evening a gendarme heard the light footsteps of two men coming carefully towards him. Without warning, he opened fire.

Kapetan George, who was leading the way, was hit and fell to the ground wounded. Without firing a shot, the accompanying guerrilla fled the scene. *Kapetan* George, unable to pick up his gun, began to shout obscenities at the gendarmes, who opened fire again, finishing him off with a burst from a machine gun.

Early the next morning, *Kapetan* George's body was taken to Kastelli and put on public display. He was wearing an old army tunic, a coarse woollen vest, army trousers that had been repaired, traditional Cretan high boots and a greatcoat. His knapsack was full of hand grenades and ammunition and he was armed with a German rifle and a pistol.

From Kastelli the body was taken through the villages to Canea. At each village a stop was made and the gendarmes encouraged the villagers to spit on *Kapetan* George's corpse. In Canea the body was put on display at the Kladissos Bridge for several days.

Four days after *Kapetan* George was killed, Mihali Boloudakis, Argiris Baras and seventeen-year-old Maria Boraki were in a hide-out close to Meskla, where several of the inhabitants remained sympathetic to the guerrillas and continued to provide them with food. Boloudakis had served as a gendarme from 1933-35, and had taken to the mountains just before the battle in Samaria Gorge. Baras was an army deserter from Agios Nikolaos and originally from Khalkidhiki. Boraki's father had been killed fighting in the Battle of Crete and her whole family had been loyal supporters of ELAS. Several members of her family were now in prison or exile for rendering assistance to the Democratic Army and Maria Boraki had taken to the mountains the previous year to be with her elder brother.

Earlier that day a patrol of gendarmes had begun a search in the vicinity of Meskla, checking on hide-outs the guerrillas were suspected of using. As the gendarmes proceeded up a track one of them spotted the three guerrillas. Both sides opened fire simultaneously.

Boloudakis and his comrades, outnumbered by at least three to one, attempted to escape but were unable to shake off the patrol. The battle raged as the gendarmes pursued the trio in the darkness. It was several hours before the firing ceased and the patrol came across Boraki's body. From the amount of blood found in the area it was clear that at least one of the other guerrillas had been seriously wounded. Boraki was the fourth guerrilla to be killed that week and her body was taken to Canea and strung up beside that of *Kapetan* George on the Kladissos Bridge.

A month later, 42-year-old Mihali Boloudakis gave himself up to Colonel Vardoulakis. The surrender was arranged after negotiations between Boloudakis' relatives and the colonel and took place just outside Canea. The prisoner was taken to the police station and that evening gave an interview to a member of the local press.

Boloudakis was freshly shaven, dressed in clean clothes and in good spirits, despite having lost the use of his right arm. On the night of the clash with the gendarmes a bullet had gone clean through his arm and Boloudakis described how he had treated the wound himself with sulphonamides to prevent infection. He had hardly eaten for the last two weeks, he said, as he lived a solitary life in hiding, having lost contact with all his comrades and had no friends to help him. He had finally decided to surrender after his vision became blurred. His wound had been tended to in prison and for dinner he had eaten two large platefuls of meat and potatoes. With a smile, he added that he had been given as much bread as he wanted and a tumbler of wine.

Boloudakis explained that he had taken to the mountains the previous year to avoid persecution in his village. At first the food supply for the rebels was quite good, he said, provisions coming regularly from the town in addition to the food that was collected from the villages. After the guerrillas' defeat in the Samaria Gorge the villagers had, out of fear, stopped supplying them with food and the provisions coming from the town had dried up completely. After the death of George Tsitilos, Boloudakis continued, the guerrillas had split into smaller groups and had lost contact with each other. Consequently he was unable to give any information on the whereabouts of the guerrillas or even any indication of exactly how many were still in hiding.

His former comrades never condemned Boloudakis for surrendering. They accepted that he had been forced to give himself up because his serious wound needed proper medical attention and, having surrendered, he did not betray any hide-out or name any of his helpers to the authorities. In fact, none of those who were to give themselves up in the coming years came in for criticism from their comrades. After enduring so much hardship hiding in the mountains for so long, several were suffering from medical conditions which made surrender their only feasible option.

On 29 December 1949, another guerrilla, Constantine Markakis, surrendered to the authorities. Markakis was wanted for desertion from the army and, among other crimes, for taking part, the previous year, in the attack on the Prasses bus in which five passengers had been killed. His relatives had been in contact with Colonel Vardoulakis and an agreement had been reached whereby, in return for giving himself up, Markakis would receive a reduced prison sentence and his mother, who was being held in Firka prison, would be released.

As the weather deteriorated that winter, the guerrillas were driven down from the mountains to seek shelter at lower altitudes. In early January 1950, Christos Boloudakis, Haralambos Belesis and Yanni Panteliadis made their way by night to the outskirts of the village of Malaxa, above Souda Bay. They planned to spend the daylight hours hiding nearby before continuing to their destination, where some of their comrades were in hiding.

Unfamiliar with the district they were moving through, they were still looking for a place to hide at sunrise and were spotted by two young shepherd boys who were out early with their flocks. The three guerrillas took the boys prisoner and led them towards Agia Marina, a church below the village.

On the way, one of the young shepherds managed to escape and ran to Malaxa to raise the alarm. A telephone call was made to Canea and Lt Colonel Voutirakis set out for Agia Marina in charge of a large force of gendarmes. The brother of the young shepherd being held by the guerrillas mobilised the local Home Guard and set off for Agia Marina without waiting for Voutirakis or other units of the Home Guard, which were already on their way from neighbouring villages.

The Malaxa Home Guard reached the church to find the three guerrillas hiding amongst the plane trees. Shooting broke out and it was almost half an hour before the gendarmes and Home Guard reinforcements arrived. By that time the battle was over. The young shepherd who had been taken hostage was found unharmed beside the bodies of two dead guerrillas; the third guerrilla had escaped.

Both the dead guerrillas were dressed in tattered army uniforms but their footwear was in good condition. Christos Boloudakis was wearing a new pair of traditional Cretan high boots and Belesis had on a new pair of army boots. A German rifle and pistol were found beside Boloudakis. Belesis had a pistol and an English rifle, which was later proved, from its serial number, to have belonged to one of the gendarmes who had recently been killed while guarding the Kladissos

Bridge. Several documents were found in Boloudakis' knapsack but as neither guerrilla was in possession of any food the authorities concluded that the guerrillas were starving and had come to the area in search of provisions.

Both the bodies were taken to Kladissos Bridge where they were strung up for public display. Since he had killed his father and godfather Christos Boloudakis had been regarded as something of a monster, greatly despised and feared by citizens of Canea. Belesis had worked as an editor of the Dimokratia before the newspaper was closed down. He later became a leading member of the spy network in town before taking to the mountains. After twenty-four hours on public display the two corpses were buried beside the river.

It was three days after the encounter at Malaxa that a search party caught up with Panteliadis. Yanni Panteliadis was a Pontic Greek from Trabzon who had arrived in Canea with his family in 1938 at the age of eighteen. He spoke Greek with a heavy accent and was also fluent in Russian and German. His father was a confectioner and Panteliadis had helped his father in the family business. During the occupation he had joined EPON and took to the mountains to join the guerrillas in 1947.

After his escape from Malaxa, Panteliadis had made his way westwards and had just settled down to spend the day hiding in a clump of carob trees near Vandes when a patrol of gendarmes spotted him. The sergeant in charge of the patrol called on him to surrender but Panteliadis' response was to take a pot shot at the sergeant. After exchanging fire with the gendarmes for fifteen minutes Panteliadis made a run for it but was shot and killed before he could get very far. His body was taken to the Kladissos Bridge and put on display until his identification was confirmed. He was later buried beside the Kladissos.

On the same day that Panteliadis was killed, Harilaos Psillakis surrendered to the authorities. Psillakis was from Lakki and since the end of the German occupation had taken a leading part in publishing propaganda for the KKE. Life as a fugitive on the run had seriously damaged his health, both physically and mentally, and he was encouraged by his brother to surrender. Some of his relatives contacted Colonel Vardoulakis and received assurances that Psillakis would be well treated if he gave himself up. Convinced that it was futile to remain in hiding, Psillakis turned himself in to the police station in Canea.

Five days later Psillakis signed a letter, published in the local newspaper, appealing to his comrades in the mountains to surrender. He assured them that he had been well treated by the authorities and had been given everything within reason he requested. The civil war was over, he said, and they should not sacrifice themselves in vain.

Colonel Vardoulakis added his voice to that of Psillakis'. He assured the guerrillas still in hiding that they had nothing to fear if they gave themselves up and implored them to follow Psillakis' example and surrender. It was only a matter of time, he said, before all the guerrillas would be captured or killed and by surrendering they would spare their families and friends much hardship and suffering, especially those believed to be sheltering the guerrillas.

True to his word, Colonel Vardoulakis continued to round up friends and relatives of the remaining guerrillas. Three weeks after Psillakis' surrender, the mother and two brothers of Georgia Skevaki were arrested and sentenced to deportation for one year.

Less than a week later, on 16 February 1950, Georgia Skevaki and her companion, Xenoula Athanasaki, were betrayed as they passed the afternoon hiding in a house in the hamlet of Lardas, near Kastelli. Despite each of them being armed with a rifle and a pistol, they were given no opportunity to put up any resistance when a gendarme patrol burst in on them. They were found to be in possession of a stack of communist propaganda, and some papers and a diary were discovered in Skevaki' knapsack.

The two women were taken to Kastelli for the night. The following day they were moved to Canea. Their capture had been announced on the radio the previous evening and a large crowd had gathered outside the prison gates, curious to get a good look at the two captives as they arrived. Both women were wearing shabby army uniforms and old, worn-out army boots and glowered at the crowd as they entered the prison.

From the time of their arrest the pair had been uncooperative, and once inside the prison declared that they would go on a hunger strike and refuse all food they were offered. Skevaki insisted that she wished to be allowed to die, the sooner the better, but after three days, nineteen-year-old Athanasaki changed her mind and began to accept food.

At the request of the local press an interview was arranged with Athanasaki. A journalist arrived to meet her one morning and described the prisoner as looking well, with red cheeks and plaited hair. For the interview she was smartly dressed in a skirt and bright red cardigan zipped up to the neck. However, the journalist was to find her quite hostile and unwilling to answer his questions.

Asked about the aims of the guerrilla army, Athanasaki replied that she did not know much about politics. She had taken to the mountains to join her brother, she said, because she was afraid of being arrested and did not want to go to prison. She had committed no crimes and therefore had no reason to regret her decision and nothing for which to repent. She gave the journalist no more information. To all other questions she answered that she did not know, could not tell or did not understand.

However, as time went on Athanasaki had a change of heart. A month later a letter signed by her and addressed to the guerrillas was published in the local press. Athanasaki told her former comrades that immediately after her arrest she had been deeply suspicious of her captors but had been well treated by them and had consequently changed her point of view. She now agreed that the guerrillas had nothing to fear if they surrendered and urged them to do so.

Several of those still on the run were hiding in the Kefalas/ Kokkino Horio/ Plaka area where they enjoyed the support of many of the locals, who gave them all the help they could. Villagers who were not sympathetic turned a deaf ear when the village dogs barked in the night at figures moving in the darkness. In the morning they ignored the footprints that had been made through newly-ploughed fields and signs that the wells had been used overnight. Apart from the need for drinking water, wells were a good place for the guerrillas to have a wash.

For their own peace of mind, the guerrillas were compelled to discover hiding places that had never previously been used by men

The Eagles of Crete

on the run. Once a local got to know of a cave or hiding place they were using it was necessary to move to another. This was to ensure that the local could not be tempted by a reward or, if arrested on suspicion of helping the guerrillas, could not be made to talk and so betray them. The guerrillas were always on the lookout for new hide-outs.

One locality in particular used by the guerrillas was the stretch of wild, remote coastline between Kefalas and Cape Drapanos. In places, the cliffs along the seashore were almost sheer and the guerrillas had discovered a few useful hide-outs that were not visible from the sea by exploring every square metre of the area. Often the approaches to the cave entrances were so dangerous that the guerrillas were confident that search parties would not attempt to approach them.

There were a few caves at sea level that the guerrillas occasionally used. One drawback to these caves was that search parties could arrive by sea without warning and take the guerrillas by surprise. This problem was solved in one of the very large caves by the sea, the Anifanti cave below Drapanos, where, after hours of exploring, the guerrillas discovered a small opening that led into an inner chamber that would be impossible for gendarmes to find on a routine search.

All caves by the sea were miserable places to be hiding in during a storm, when the deafening wind whistled through the caves for days on end. In stormy weather, guerrillas in the sea-level caves were often unable to leave while the waves beat against the rocks outside and water occasionally came into the cave itself. However, one advantage of the caves by the sea was that it was easier for the guerrillas to dispose of excrement. When hiding nearer villages it was difficult to dispose of human waste, which always had to be buried some way from the hide-out to avoid giving away their presence.

At their meeting in the mountains in the summer of 1950, the fugitives had a long discussion on how best to rejuvenate the political party in the town. Several of the guerrillas were keen to move their hide-out from the remote countryside to facilitate this regeneration.

It was finally agreed that 26-year-old Eleftherios Iliakis should go into Canea and re-establish contact with the few loyal comrades who were not in prison. Iliakis was almost completely unknown in town and could therefore move around far more easily than most of the others. The mission to Canea was a dangerous one but Iliakis willingly agreed to go and walked into Canea in July. He was supplied with a list of people to contact, and one of his jobs was to find a safe house in town that the guerrillas could use. A rendezvous with Kokovlis was arranged near the monastery of Agia Triada on the Akrotiri for a few weeks later.

Kokovlis planned to move his own hide-out to the Akrotiri, calculating that the peninsula, which was very close to Canea, was possibly the safest area for them to use. The Akrotiri was connected to the rest of Crete by a small neck of land and should the authorities learn that guerrillas were hiding in the area it would be a simple matter to close off the isthmus and search for them at their leisure. As it was such a potentially dangerous place, it was also one of the areas in which the authorities would least suspect the guerrillas to be hiding.

One night, soon after Iliakis had set off for Canea, Nikos Kokovlis and Argiro Polychronaki went down to a beach near Plaka. Polychronaki, a former member of EPON from Drakona, had taken to the mountains in 1947 to be with her brother, Constantine, and had chosen to remain with the guerrillas after her brother surrendered in 1948.

After a while, they heard the splashing of oars and a fishing boat appeared out of the darkness. The two young fishermen, Harilaos and Vassili, put in to the shore and the pair leapt aboard. In virtual silence they crossed over to the Akrotiri, keeping a careful lookout for any naval patrol boat. Having deposited their human cargo on a deserted beach, the two fishermen set off back to the other side of Souda bay, intending to do some fishing before reappearing in their village. They needed a decent catch to justify their night out at sea.

On the Akrotiri the pair made for the village of Hordaki to meet their contact, Adonis Douroundakis, a veteran of the Battle of Crete and a member of ELAS during the occupation. Douroundakis had taken no part in the civil war but they hoped he would find them a suitable hiding-place near his village. Douroundakis did not disappoint them. He knew of several caves in the hills near Hordaki where the guerrillas were able to hide and soon enlisted the help of a shepherd who was able to help in supplying the fugitives with food.

According to local legend, one of the remote caves in that region was haunted. Douroundakis led the guerrillas to this cave, which, because of its reputation, the locals rarely visited. The cave was on a steep rocky hillside and the fugitives felt it would be a safe place to hide.

One morning, however, the peace was disturbed when a man and his son were heard approaching with a donkey. They halted below the cave and, taking a shovel and sack, began to make their way up the steep slope to the cave's entrance. On the way they collected handfuls of thyme and pieces of wood.

The fugitives moved as far as they could to the back of the cave. When the two strangers arrived at the cave's entrance the man started to shovel goat dung, which was to be used as fertiliser, into the sack while the boy used the thyme and wood to light a fire. The guerrillas remained motionless but before long the light from the flames gave them away.

When the man and his son saw silhouettes at the back of the cave they screamed out in terror. Kokovlis stepped forward and, having reassured them that they were not ghosts, sat the man and his son down and explained that reprisals would be taken against the whole village should the authorities ever learn that guerrillas had been hiding near Hordaki. Despite promises from the pair that they would tell nobody of the guerrillas' presence it was obviously not safe to release them before nightfall. After dusk fell the two were released and that night the fugitives moved their hide-out.

Despite this piece of bad luck, all seemed to be going as planned. Eleftherios Iliakis kept the rendezvous with Kokovlis near the monastery of Agia Triada at the pre-arranged time. He reported that he was making good progress in Canea and was confident that a safe house would soon be available. Iliakis returned to town, with the promise that Kokovlis would join him there as soon as the safe house had been organised.

At the beginning of November, Colonel Vardoulakis announced another offer of an amnesty. All guerrillas who surrendered within the next ten days were to receive a pardon for crimes committed before 1 October 1950. The colonel called on the guerrillas to cease living as outlaws and rejoin society for the sake of peace in the countryside.

The day before this amnesty expired, Eleftherios Iliakis was recognised by a fellow villager as he was walking down the street in Canea and pointed out to a police patrol. The three-man patrol, led by a corporal, caught up with Iliakis, who was unarmed, and placed him under arrest. News soon spread that a dangerous guerrilla had been arrested in town and other policemen joined the arresting party. By the time they reached the police station a lieutenant was in charge of the prisoner and the seven policemen escorting him. A large crowd of inquisitive townspeople followed them.

When interrogated by the police, Iliakis claimed that he had been hiding alone in a cave near Galatas and had recently come to Canea to find a hiding place. He had had no intention of surrendering and was awaiting a general amnesty for all political prisoners, not just an amnesty for the fugitives in Crete. Iliakis was later sentenced to four terms of life imprisonment.

One of those asked by Douroundakis to help the fugitives was Kiriakos Stratigakis, a former member of ELAS. Stratigakis was well known for his leftwing views and Douroundakis knew he could be trusted to keep his mouth shut, even if he was unwilling to help. When approached with the suggestion that he help two wanted fugitives, Stratigakis accepted without hesitation.

Stratigakis lived with his wife and three children on a smallholding 100 metres outside the hamlet of Plakoures, eight kilometres from Canea. The house in which he lived was known as Troulitis and was owned by his sister who had married and emigrated to the USA many years earlier. The neighbourhood around Plakoures was much more built-up than any area previously used by the guerrillas, but Stratigakis was confident that he could successfully hide Kokovlis and Polychronaki.

The Eagles of Crete

Stratigakis proposed that the fugitives hide in his barn. At night the barn housed a donkey and two goats but these were put out to pasture during the daytime. There were two windows at the back that were closed all day and two at the front which were left open. A fly screen over the windows obscured the view inside and bales of hay were placed so as to block the lower half of the windows completely. Two large wine barrels provided cover behind which the fugitives could safely sit on bales of hay all day. There were plenty of sacks and tarpaulins, used during the olive-picking season, which made comfortable bedding. Compared to some of the hide-outs in the mountains, the barn provided an agreeable place to hide and Kokovlis and Polychronaki were careful to avoid removing any dust or spiders' webs in order not to arouse suspicions that somebody might be living there.

Now that a safe hiding place was established, the work of developing the political organisation in the town began. The first person to be approached for help was Athina Tsangaraki, the sister of the guerrilla, Dimitri, who had been with Kokovlis when he was killed in the White Mountains the previous year. Twenty-year-old Athina had moved from her village to Canea and had found work in a bookshop. Stratigakis' wife, Georgia, successfully approached her while she was alone in the shop and she agreed to meet Polychronaki.

One evening later that week, Kiriakos Stratigakis guided Polychronaki into Canea, walking some distance ahead so that the two would not be seen together. On arrival at Athina Tsangaraki's small house, in the suburb of Agios Ioannis, he left the women to talk together.

The meeting was a great success. Tsangaraki readily accepted the request to hide Polychronaki in her home from time to time to enable her to make contacts in Canea. She would also help to find other hiding places in town and, thanks to her job in the bookshop, would be able to guarantee a constant supply of paper, stencils and ink for use in printing communist propaganda. After careful searching she managed to find the fugitives a second-hand typewriter. Back at Troulitis, Kokovlis rigged up a primitive mimeograph and soon had the production of a news-sheet, *Popular Unity*, up and running

The next person to be approached for help was Stratigakis' elder brother, Ilarion, who had been an ELAS reservist during the occupation. Ilarion was acquainted with Kokovlis before the occupation and willingly accepted his brother's suggestion that he meet up with him. To prevent Ilarion suspecting that fugitives were hiding in the vicinity of Plakoures, the meeting took place in a forest near Profitis Ilias, close to Canea.

On a chilly autumn evening, Kiriakos guided Kokovlis to the meeting place and left him there. Ilarion arrived a short time later. It had been almost a decade since the pair had last met but Ilarion had no hesitation in agreeing to make further contacts for Kokovlis and to help with circulating the news-sheet, *Popular Unity*.

Over the winter of 1950-51 the organisation in Canea increased its numbers and went from strength to strength. Several hide-outs and useful contacts were established in the town. One of the first to help was Sophia Hatzigrigori, the sister of the myopic lawyer, Stavros, who had been killed in the mountains two years earlier. Her house was well-known to the security police so was impractical as a hide-out, but Hatzigrigori provided Kokovlis with workman's overalls to enable him to walk the streets of Canea in the early morning without arousing suspicion; to Polychronaki she gave a wristwatch to ensure she was punctual at her meetings in town.

Another to offer help was a relative of Polychronaki's who had a house on the outskirts of Canea. Polychronaki was able to hide in her relative's hencoop during the daytime when the hens were released into the field. An alternative hiding place was a huge, hollow olive tree on one of the nearby terraces.

Kokovlis had several old friends who readily offered their help when it was requested. One of these was a former neighbour who took on the task of collecting clothing and financial contributions, ostensibly for the KKE inmates in Kalami prison. Another was a member of the KKE who had a shop selling electrical appliances in the centre of town, opposite Canea Town Hall. This shop soon became the distribution centre for *Popular Unity* as well as the dropping off place for messages that the fugitives in Canea prefecture wished to pass to each other.

Douroundakis had performed a very useful service for Kokovlis by putting him in contact with Stratigakis and ensuring a safe hide-out near to Canea. Three years after Kokovlis and Polychronaki established themselves at Troulitis, Douroundakis became a monk at the nearby monastery of Agia Triada. For years afterwards he would occasionally meet the fugitives late at night and provide them with money. Throughout all those years they never told him where they were hiding, and he never asked.

Chapter 12
Decision to Disband

The authorities were completely baffled as to where the fugitives had gone. For over a year they had shown no sign of life and every indication was that they had moved out of the mountains, where regular patrols found no trace of them, and were being sheltered by a secret organisation in a remote part of the prefecture. Suspicion fell upon certain villages in Apokoronas, especially the area around Gavalohori where three of the fugitives had grown up. In August 1951 another roundup of suspects began and 51 arrests were made.

Half a dozen of those arrested were believed to be the ringleaders who had direct contact with the guerrillas, while others provided food, money and information on the movements of search parties. Several had served prison terms and periods in exile and a few had signed declarations of repentance and received amnesties. A large supply of food was found in one house in Douliana and the authorities suspected that the guerrillas used another house in the village as a regular meeting place. Many of those arrested were found in possession of communist propaganda and confessed their guilt. They all received prison sentences and the guerrillas hiding in the area lost some of their most important helpers.

The leftists in Crete came under such intense pressure in this period that one of them decided to leave his island home for Athens. Kostas Kasiotakis, a farmer from Kefalas and former member of ELAS, had been arrested and imprisoned for possession of communist literature. On his release, Kasiotakis found he was under constant surveillance by the security police and life was made difficult for him. He eventually left for Athens, where he ran a kiosk. His departure from Crete turned out to be a blessing in disguise for the fugitives. In Athens, Kasiotakis made contact with the underground KKE movement and was able to pass messages between the KKE leadership in the capital and the fugitives in Crete. This contact was to be invaluable in the years to come.

Another development which affected the fugitives was the formation in Athens, in August 1951, of a new political party, the United Democratic Left (EDA). EDA leaders proposed an amnesty for all political prisoners and legalisation of the KKE. Radio Free Greece, which transmitted broadcasts into Greece from behind the Iron Curtain, gave its blessing to EDA.

In the 1951 elections EDA won just over 10% of the vote nationally and ten of the two hundred and fifty seats in Parliament. No party won an overall majority and a coalition of General Plastiras' National Progressive Centre Union and the Liberals formed a government.

After four years in hiding, Yanni Manousakas was seriously ill. Since the death of George Romanias, Manousakas had been living the solitary life of a fugitive, suspicious of anybody he met in the mountains. He had a huge reward on his head and only accepted food from shepherds that he knew well. Day by day he became more paranoid and unwilling to trust the few people with whom he came into contact. It was his illness that eventually drove him from the mountains.

Manousakas walked for two nights to reach his aunt's house in the village of Zouridi, very close to his native village of Agios Konstantinos. His mother and sister were staying with his aunt and the three of them were shocked at his appearance. They worked hard for two days digging a hole in their barn that was big enough for him to crawl into if a search party came looking for him. Once inside the hole he could pull down a bale of hay over the entrance to completely block it and conceal himself from view. Manousakas spent three months in his aunt's barn and passed his time reading and writing.

Manousakas's health, however, showed little improvement so via his mother he sent a note to a relative who had a house just outside the village. In the note Manousakas explained that he was unwell and needed a place to hide. The relative had spent several years in the USA before returning to his village to marry and was known to be an anticommunist. At the same time, as one of his own kin, Manousakas knew that his relative would not betray him to the police, even if he chose not to assist him.

Manousakas arrived at his cousin's home barefoot. He was clearly in poor health and the cousin took pity on him and immediately offered his help. Manousakas enjoyed three months in his new, comfortable hide-out and each evening the cousin was able to recount news and gossip from the local *kapheneion* and engage in political discussions with his guest. For the moment Manousakas was happy to remain where he was and, when he heard that the other guerrillas were trying to find him, let it be known through his mother and relatives that they knew nothing of his whereabouts and presumed him to be dead.

By October 1952, Manousakas was suffering from tuberculosis. With no other option, he persuaded a trusted friend to go to Canea and contact a known police informer and arrange his surrender. A few days later Manousakas made the trip to Canea by car and turned himself in. The police took the credit for having Manousakas in custody and announced to the press, without giving any details, that they had captured Yanni Manousakas, who they described as a dangerous communist, in a well-planned ambush.

On the day that Manousakas was making his way to Canea to surrender, eight villagers from Plaka were arrested for giving assistance to the guerrillas. Six of the eight were fishermen and, by chance, included one of the men who had ferried the guerrillas over to the Akrotiri two years earlier. Two of those arrested were females: one was twenty years old and the other the forty-year-old wife of the local priest.

The arrests followed the discovery of a hitherto unknown cave beside the sea, about two kilometres north of Plaka by some young boys who had taken a boat along the coast from Almirida one morning to shoot pigeons. Keeping close to the shore, they had followed a narrow inlet at a spot known locally as Palomidi, and this led to a cave, that was not visible from the sea. An examination of the cave showed signs of occupation, and they quickly rowed back to Almirida to report their find.

At first the gendarmerie tried to keep the discovery of the cave secret and prepared an ambush for any fugitives who might return to it.

The press was not informed but a rumour that the hide-out had been found spread rapidly and plans for an ambush were abandoned.

Inside the cave were three bedrolls, which had been placed over some linoleum to protect them from the damp. The cave was well provided with cooking utensils, an abundance of food, especially spaghetti, several litres of olive oil, two oil lamps and dozens of church candles. There were also some army uniforms, a rifle and ammunition, shaving implements, a pile of printed documents, handwritten KKE proclamations and some English cigarettes. At the back of the cave a large rock covered a hole that led to another smaller cave where more documents were found. A cooking pot contained a meal of aubergines that was beginning to rot, suggesting that the guerrillas had left the cave at least two days earlier.

As the cave was not visible from dry land and was concealed by a sheer, smooth overhanging rock, several metres high, the gendarmes decided that access from the landward side would be impossible. They failed to notice the cracks that had carefully been made in the rock with a chisel, large enough only for toeholds at the bottom but with larger holes at the top. These small holes enabled the guerrillas to make the very risky climb in and out of the cave at will, their boots hung around their necks by the laces, and their use of the cave was kept secret from the fishermen at nearby Plaka. However, convinced that the cave could only be approached from the sea, the gendarmes arrested the fishermen, several of whom were suspected of being communist sympathisers.

The discovery of the cave was followed by an appeal from the chief of police asking for the help of all law-abiding citizens in wiping out the remaining guerrillas. These fugitives, he said, were clearly being fed and sheltered by locals who were committing an act of treason against their country and all those who considered themselves patriots should work with the authorities to eradicate the few dangerous communists still in hiding.

As usual this appeal fell on deaf ears and it was going to be almost a year before another fugitive fell into the hands of the authorities.

In October 1952 the thirteen fugitives still at liberty in western Crete assembled in the White Mountains, high above Kambi. Two of the thirteen were women and four were non-Cretans. Contact had finally been made with the two men who had been on the run in Kissamos following the battle in the Samaria Gorge. Stamatis Mariolis, one of the aircraftsmen who had helped in the capture of Maleme airfield, and Yanni Nikolopoulos, a deserter from the Agios Nikolaos garrison, met up with their surviving comrades for the first time in over four years.

A third fugitive, Manoli Frangiadakis, an army deserter from Agios Nikolaos, had been killed in a fight with Yanni Nikolopoulos the previous year. Nikolopoulos gave the assembly his version of the incident. The pair of them, he said, had gone to the home of a reliable comrade in Milonou one night to collect some supplies and while there they had a heated discussion on politics. Frangiadakis had the better of the argument and Nikolopoulos became so angry that he pulled out a knife and stabbed Frangiadakis to death.

Two other guerrillas, Xenophon Kodonidis and Stefanos Koutsoupakis, who had taken to the mountains in 1946, had disappeared completely and were never heard of again. Their former comrades speculated that the two men, who were not hiding together, may have died of illness in a remote cave or had fallen into a deep ravine while walking at night. Even the authorities were not aware of their deaths: in the Nea Epohi of 6 February 1960 the two men were included on a wanted list, with the reward for their capture increased.

For three days the fugitives discussed the political situation and the forthcoming General Election. Having agreed a time and place for their next meeting they returned to their various hideouts.

Kokovlis and Polychronaki continued their work, publishing their communist news-sheet regularly and increasing their circle of contacts. Several of their new helpers were young relatives and friends of those who had taken part in the civil war and included a nephew of Manoli Pissadakis. Kiriakos Stratigakis' eighteen-year-old son, Harilaos, was let in on the secret that two fugitives were hiding in the family barn and soon became a trusted messenger who, because of his youth, was above suspicion. Despite the obvious danger, Kokovlis made frequent trips into Canea to make contact with old friends who were likely to provide assistance if asked. Polychronaki was able to move around

Canea by borrowing a young child from a supporter. Nobody suspected a woman with a young child would be carrying out work for the KKE.

On 19 February 1953, to mark the tenth anniversary of the founding of EPON, the network of communist sympathisers went to work in Canea. Using the darkness, they scattered hundreds of communist proclamations and handbills in the deserted streets in the centre of town and on the road to Souda. The sacrifices made by members of EPON, EAM and ELAS during the occupation were commemorated and all citizens were urged to create a new Patriotic Front and oppose the government's pro-US policies. Gendarmes and soldiers were encouraged to sabotage military installations. The same evening, handwritten proclamations supporting the KKE were scattered throughout several villages and anti-American and anti-British slogans were daubed on walls.

On a chilly night in late November 1953, a gendarme patrol made its way to a cave at Sopoto, near Kaina. By chance, Angelis Iliakis had decided to use this cave as a temporary refuge for the night and was sitting outside it smoking a cigarette. It was the light from the cigarette in the darkness that the gendarmes spotted from a distance. They approached quietly but as they drew closer Iliakis heard them and threw a grenade, which exploded without causing any injury.

Intermittent firing went on throughout the night. In the early morning a senior gendarme officer arrived to take charge of the operation. The officer appealed to Iliakis to surrender; in reply Iliakis demanded an amnesty.

At noon the gendarmes, in an attempt to smoke Iliakis out, started a fire close to the entrance of the cave. His lungs bursting, Iliakis was forced to come to the cave entrance for air. As soon as he came into view the gendarmes opened fire, killing him instantly. His corpse was taken to Dikastirion Square in Canea where it was strung up on display.

Further south, that winter, Argiris Baras was making his way along a remote path one night near Voutas to the home of one of his supporters when he was spotted by a search party of gendarmes. By chance, the gendarmes had set up an ambush on the precise route Baras was taking. The gendarmes waited, but as Baras drew closer his suspicions were aroused and he tried to make a run for it.

The gendarmes opened fire, wounding Baras in the arm. In his haste to escape in the darkness, Baras, who was wearing sandals soled with car tyres, stumbled into a small ravine, fracturing his hip. Unable to escape he fought off the gendarmes for almost six hours, during which time he burnt all the papers he had with him. At 6 am, short on ammunition and in great pain, he surrendered.

Baras was taken to the clinic in Kandanos where he was given medical attention before being transferred to Canea prison. When questioned, he refused to confess to anything or to give away any information on the whereabouts of his comrades. Frustrated in their hopes that Baras would lead them to other fugitives, the security police beat him severely.

Ten weeks after his arrest Baras was brought to trial. Two fellow prisoners helped to shoulder him into the courtroom and put him into a chair. Before a jury was selected his lawyer asked for a postponement on the grounds that Baras would be unable to follow the trial properly as he was still in pain from his injuries. Two doctors were brought, the courtroom cleared and the examination made. The doctors decided that Baras was too ill to follow proceedings and the trial was postponed.

One of the three non-Cretans still on the run in Crete was George Korakas. Born in Asia Minor, Korakas was orphaned when he was four years old. As a young man he arrived in Canea where he worked as a farm labourer before being called up for national service. When war broke out, he served on the Albanian front, and during the occupation took to the mountains with ELAS in the Peloponnese. Soon after his return to Crete, Korakas joined the guerrilla army and after its defeat spent much of his time in hiding in Kissamos.

After some years of life on the run, he became seriously ill. Too exhausted to walk far, he was unable to maintain contact with the few people who were willing to provide him with food. In order to regain his health, Korakas was faced with the choice of surrendering or seeing a doctor. Fortunately, Korakas did know a doctor for whom he had worked before the war, but the doctor was a nationalist.

Doctor Stilianos Georgilas was eighty years old and had retired to a house by the sea, in a hamlet close to Maleme. Korakas, clearly unwell, arrived at Doctor Georgilas' house one evening after dark and was admitted to see him. It had been over fifteen years since they had last met but the doctor recognised him. To the fugitive's relief, Doctor Georgilas told him that despite their opposing political views he would take care of him until he was better. He insisted that Korakas spend the rest of the night in his home.

Korakas remained at the doctor's home for a few days, resting in the storeroom amongst the barrels of wine and olive oil, but there were frequent visitors to the house. Doctor Georgilas owned another small house by the beach nearby that had been badly damaged by the bombing in the war and had not yet been repaired. It was now used for storing hay and agricultural produce for a few months in the summer and Georgilas suggested that Korakas use this ruin as a hide-out. Korakas spent the first few days in his new hiding place digging a hole in the floor. In the event that he was surprised by a search party, Korakas was confident that he could use this hole, covered over by a piece of asbestos, to escape detection.

Korakas soon recovered from his illness and the ruined house provided a perfect hide-out for him. However, it was in a more populated area than he was used to using. He had hardly been there a month when a farm worker spotted him as he left his refuge one evening before it was dark. The farm worker suspected the stranger was a fugitive and ran to the gendarme post at Maleme.

Korakas was sitting among some bushes fifty metres from his hide-out when he heard the patrol arrive, but he successfully made his getaway. The patrol found the remains of a recently cooked meal in the ruined house, along with Korakas' few possessions. As the property was owned by Dr Georgilas, a prominent member of the community and a well-known nationalist, the police were unwilling to believe that he had any personal knowledge of Korakas' presence in the building.

The Eagles of Crete

When questioned, the family claimed that the house was far enough from their home for them not to know that a wanted man was using it as a refuge. The police did not believe this story and arrested the doctor's son. Several locals were also taken into custody, including a builder who was suspected of excavating the hole in the floor.

A week after these arrests, there was a public outcry when Dr Georgilas was arrested. In the police station Dr Georgilas confessed to having treated Korakas and stated that as a doctor and a human being he had no choice in the matter. After a week in jail the doctor was released out of consideration for his age and the respect felt for him in the community.

Another of the fugitives to have a lucky escape that winter was "Stefanos", as he was known to those hiding him in Kissamos. A patrol from Kastelli had come across the fugitive one night and opened fire without warning. The fugitive was wounded but escaped and the authorities were confident that he would die of his wounds. A short time later, seventeen arrests were made of locals who were suspected of helping this particular fugitive. Most confessed to helping Stefanos and admitted that they had treated the fugitive for the injuries he had received in his encounter with the patrol.

A month later Stefanos was discovered in his hide-out in a wooded gorge near Deliana by some local villagers. He was immediately surrounded by the local Home Guard while a message was sent to the nearest gendarme post for assistance. Reinforcements came from every direction and, after putting up a brief resistance, the fugitive threw down his gun and surrendered.

Later that day the authorities announced that they had arrested Dimitri Kontokonstantis, an Athenian who already had a price on his head for murder before arriving in Crete in 1946. When news of Kontokonstantis' arrest reached the fugitives in their various hide-outs in Canea they were puzzled as they knew that Kontokonstantis had been executed by a group of guerrillas when he had tried to surrender five years earlier.

Argiris Baras had recovered from his injuries sufficiently in time to stand trial with the fugitive known as Stefanos. Both were accused of joining an armed insurrection against the state and several gendarmes gave evidence against them. When Baras was given the opportunity to speak in his defence he claimed that he was guilty of political not criminal acts and proceeded to give the court a political lecture. The judge reminded Baras that he was on trial and should therefore concentrate on the specific accusations made against him. Baras replied that the biggest criminal in the court was the judge himself.

Following this outburst the judge sentenced Baras to a year in prison for contempt of court. Unmoved, Baras continued with his speech, admitting that he had been a member of the guerrilla army and stating that he was proud of the part he had played in the civil war in Crete. Baras was found guilty of armed insurrection and given a life sentence.

When "Stefanos" had the opportunity to speak he announced that he was not Dimitri Kontokonstantis but Yanni Nikolopoulos, an Athenian who had come to Crete as a national serviceman in 1947. He protested that he was innocent of all the crimes he was accused of and was only guilty of desertion. The police, he said, had named him as Kontokonstantis in order to collect the enormous reward of sixty million drachmas that was outstanding for his arrest. Nikolopoulos was found guilty of armed insurrection and sentenced to life imprisonment. An investigation was ordered to establish the exact identity of the defendant.

The newspapers took up the story and the Chief of Police in Canea was forced to make a statement. He insisted that Nikolopoulos had the identity card of Dimitri Kontokonstantis in his possession at the time of his arrest. While being taken into custody the fugitive had claimed to be Kontokonstantis and he had signed the statement he had made to the police in the name of Kontokonstantis. Even his lawyer had believed his client to be Kontokonstantis. The amount of the reward was nowhere near the figure given by Nikolopoulos and, in any case, was payable to the Home Guard and villagers of Deliana and not to members of the police force. The Chief of Police agreed that a mistake had been made and the fugitive in question was, in fact, Yanni Nikolopoulos.

In Rethymnon and Heraklion prefectures there were still five fugitives at large, including the most senior member of the KKE on the island, George Kontokotsos. Born in Grevena, Kontokotsos had been exiled to Gavdos during the Metaxas regime and during the occupation had been in charge of EPON throughout Crete. The guerrillas in Canea had been unable to contact him after the death of George Tsitilos when they were seeking a new leader. Following the arrest of Doctor Siganos and the death of Vangelio Kladou in 1949, Kontokotsos was the only remaining member of the central committee of the KKE in Crete at liberty.

The other four fugitives in Rethymnon and Heraklion were Yanni Dakanalis, Kostas Patramanis and the Sbokos brothers, Constantine and George. All of these were from the Anogia area and had joined Podias in the brief rebellion in eastern Crete in 1947.

The first of these to fall into the hands of the authorities was Yanni Dakanalis, who was betrayed to the police for the reward of ten million drachmas. A lieutenant colonel from Heraklion led the large force that made the arrest at Gournes in the early hours of a July morning in 1954.

A month after the capture of Dakanalis, George Kontokotsos walked into the police station in Heraklion and surrendered. A few days later, twenty suspects were rounded up and charged with aiding the two men.

There followed a trial that lasted just one day, at the end of which Dakanalis was sentenced to three years in jail and Kontokotsos to two. Kontokotsos received the lighter sentence in view of the fact that he had surrendered. Those who had helped them to evade capture received sentences of between six and eighteen months.

Three months later, two gendarmes were on patrol near Melambes when they saw two figures in the distance. The two men fled as the gendarmes approached and the gendarmes gave chase, whereupon one of the men pulled out a pistol and fired, fatally wounding one of the gendarmes in the stomach. Meanwhile, other gendarmes from the station at Melambes joined in the pursuit and managed to arrest one of the men. The captured man was a resident of Melambes and he immediately confessed that he had been acting as a messenger for George Sbokos, who had escaped after firing at the gendarmes.

Search parties combed the area and were rewarded the following morning when they cornered 44-year-old Sbokos. He resisted briefly but, seeing that escape was impossible, burnt all the documents he had with him before putting his pistol to his temple and shooting himself in the head.

Thirty-three villagers were arrested on suspicion of sheltering and feeding George Sbokos, thirty of them from the village of Melambes. After a brief trial, two were jailed for three years and eight received sentences ranging from six to eighteen months. Twenty were found not guilty through lack of evidence and released.

Kostas Patramanis, a former *kapetan* with ELAS, was later betrayed, arrested and imprisoned; shortly afterwards Constantine Sbokos surrendered.

There were now just ten communist fugitives at liberty in Crete, all based in the most westerly prefecture of Canea. In addition to the typewriter and mimeograph that Kokovlis and Polychronaki had on the Akrotiri there was also a typewriter and radio in the cave shared by the Lionakis brothers, Yanni and Kostas, and Pagona Kokovli on the coast to the north of Kefalas. Through their intermediaries, the fugitives were able to communicate with each other and meet up at least once a year.

But the fugitives were living in a changing world. An ambitious road-building programme had been started three or four years earlier and there were now roads to the once-remote villages of Therisso and Hora Sfakion. Work was in progress on a road from Prasses to the south coast at Sougia and the road from Lakki to Omalos was finished in the late summer of 1954. General Mandakas donated the house he owned on Omalos, which had been used by the guerrillas in the winter of 1947-48, to the Greek Mountaineering Club of Canea for use as a mountain hut. A mountain refuge was also being built at Volikas, above Kambi, for citizens of the town who wished to explore the White Mountains. The once lonely regions were being made more accessible.

The Eagles of Crete

Even more disturbing for the fugitives, in the summer of 1954 the Greek government announced that, at the request of NATO, a military airport and American base were to be built on the Akrotiri, only a few kilometres from the hide-out used by Kokovlis and Polychronaki.

In the winter of 1954-55, a plan was drawn up to remove the inhabitants of the village of Samaria to the coast. Compensation of five million drachmas was to be paid to the villagers for loss of grazing rights. It was to be several more years before this proposal was put into effect, but it was foreseen that the removal of the villagers would allow the gorge to be developed for tourism and as a national park where hunting would be banned and where the Cretan wild goat, the agrimi, could thrive. Twenty villagers of Agia Roumeli signed an undertaking to give up hunting the island's wild goats.

Official delegations were received and made welcome in Crete from both Italy and Germany. One of the aims of these delegations was to organise the recovery of the bones of their soldiers who had been killed during the occupation. A mass grave holding the remains of over a hundred of their compatriots who had been executed by the Germans was uncovered by the Italians at Patellari. The bones of another hundred Italians were found in secluded graves throughout Canea prefecture. Among other places, the Germans visited Koustogerako, where the locals escorted them on the three-hour climb up the mountain to help them retrieve the remains of soldiers who had died in an ambush in 1943.

Relations were also improving with neighbouring countries which had recently supported the communist rebels, and even Albania, which was fast becoming isolated from the rest of the world, made a gesture of reconciliation in 1956 by returning nine officers and two hundred and twenty-four Greek soldiers who had been held prisoner since the end of the civil war.

Many of those who had been imprisoned during the civil war were now being released. It was not unusual for villagers to get together and organise a petition asking for the release of a fellow villager who was being held for offences committed during the rebellion, claiming that they were young men who had been taken in by communist propaganda and were therefore not fully responsible for their actions. Xan Fielding, one of the British officers who had served in Crete during the occupation, became involved in such a case on a visit to the island in the early nineteen-fifties.

Panayiotis Tsamantis had been in prison since his arrest in 1948 and his relatives asked Fielding to attend his appeal in Canea and speak up for him. Fielding did so, reminding the court that Tsamantis had been wounded in 1944 while escorting Staff Sergeant Dudley Perkins, a New Zealander, through the White Mountains. The village priest also spoke up for Tsamantis, who was released and later emigrated to New Zealand.

There were now fewer patrols searching for the fugitives. It had become clear to the authorities that their quarry was no longer in the White Mountains but had found safe hide-outs nearer to friendly villages. As four of the ten fugitives were from Gavalohori and Kokkino Horio, a large area centred on these villages was established as a special zone, known locally as The Balkans, where a curfew was put in force. This caused some inconvenience to villagers wishing to go about their daily agricultural work but they put up with this disruption to their lives and, as usual, even those who suspected that the fugitives were in the area continued to keep these thoughts to themselves and did not betray their suspicions to the authorities.

The rewards on offer for the wanted men were increased and promises of relocation and a change of identity were given to anyone who betrayed a fugitive. Over the years the suspicion had grown amongst the guerrillas that some of their comrades who had walked into ambushes had in fact been betrayed. But the fugitives had little alternative to trusting those who helped them.

It was at the end of 1955 that George Korakas was tricked into walking into a police trap. One of his contacts had promised Korakas that he would put him in touch with a former comrade who was able and willing to provide him with a new hiding place. Korakas was to meet this old friend late one Saturday night on the outskirts of Canea and, desperate to renew the acquaintance, he kept the appointment, not suspecting that his contact had sold him out to the authorities.

Colonel Mitsou took charge of the operation to capture Korakas. Several gendarmes concealed themselves around the meeting place and the colonel hid in a ditch near to where Korakas had been told to wait. When Korakas arrived at the appointed place, Colonel Mitsou climbed out of his ditch and approached him. It was only at the last minute that Korakas realised that he had walked into a trap and by then escape was impossible. In the ensuing struggle, Colonel Mitsou received one or two bruises but he was later able to boast that he had personally arrested a dangerous fugitive.

A news blackout was imposed and the authorities refused to comment on rumours that a fugitive had been captured and was being held in solitary confinement at the police station. Four days after Korakas' arrest, newspaper reports that he was in police custody were met by Colonel Mitsou's insistence that any announcement on the arrest of fugitives in Crete would be made by the appropriate ministry in Athens.

The authorities swiftly rounded up those suspected of helping and hiding Korakas. Among those detained was the contact Korakas had used to pass notes to the other fugitives. This contact, a carpenter, had allowed his workshop to be used as a centre where couriers from the fugitives could leave and receive coded messages from each other. Although he did not know the couriers by name the carpenter knew them by sight and there was a real possibility that the network sheltering the fugitives would be exposed.

Arrests of prominent left-wingers continued throughout Canea for some time. As the police gave out no details of those arrested, representatives of the local committee of EDA made a formal complaint to the authorities. The EDA officials unsuccessfully demanded that Korakas should immediately be removed from solitary confinement, where they claimed he was being tortured to make him talk. They accused the authorities of stirring up a climate of fear and demanded that relatives of those detained should be informed of their whereabouts and the detainees themselves should be tried forthwith, if there was any evidence against them.

The situation suddenly worsened for the fugitives when the Stratigakis brothers, Kiriakos and Ilarion, were arrested. Despite the risks, Kokovlis and Polychronaki remained where they were and continued printing hundreds of proclamations, demanding the release of all those who had been arrested by the police. The names of Kiriakos and Ilarion Stratigakis were added to the list of those who, it was claimed, had been wrongfully arrested, and Kiriakos' son, Harilaos, scattered the proclamations in the centre of Canea late at night. By doing this it was hoped that the authorities would believe that those under arrest could not be responsible in any way for the communist literature on the streets of Canea, the printing and distribution of which had clearly not been interrupted.

After six months in prison, Kiriakos Stratigakis was finally brought to trial. There were no witnesses to give evidence against him and he had confessed to nothing so he was acquitted and released, along with dozens of others, including his brother, Ilarion.

Only one of the fugitives was captured during this period, betrayed in his hide-out, three months after the arrest of Korakas. Again, as with Korakas, Colonel Mitsou led the patrol that made the arrest. Having surrounded a house just outside Gerani late one night, the colonel entered the building and went straight to the trap door of the cellar. On opening it he shouted down to *Kapetan* Mihali that he knew he was hiding there and called on him to surrender. *Kapetan* Mihali came out with his hands up and was taken into custody along with the owners of the house in which he had been hiding.

Kapetan Mihali, the military commander of the guerrilla army from September 1947 to June 1948, had been sentenced to death in absentia. While awaiting trial in Kalami prison he maintained the habit of his years on the run of sleeping during the day, and spent the nights chatting to his former comrades, of whom there were several in the prison. His lawyers cleverly managed to have the accusations against him downgraded and to have his trial put off for several years. When his case eventually came to court in 1960, *Kapetan* Mihali received a short prison sentence and was released soon afterwards. In 1963, he died of ill health, which his former comrades claimed was brought on by the deprivations and hardship suffered while on the run.

The Eagles of Crete

Following the capture of *Kapetan Mihali*, Colonel Mitsou let it be known through a senior EDA activist in Canea that the government wanted to end the problem of the fugitives in Crete and offered to make a ship available that would take them to a country of their choice. The only condition insisted on by Colonel Mitsou was that all the arrangements should take place in secret as members of the government did not want to be seen to be negotiating with the fugitives.

The eight fugitives met up at a hide-out in Apokoronas to discuss the suggestion that they make a deal with the authorities and leave Greece. They were all suspicious of the scheme and rejected it, suspecting a trap. Instead, they agreed to send a message to EDA, asking for a bill to be put before Parliament requesting a general amnesty for the fugitives in Crete. The authorities turned down this proposal and the fugitives remained in their various hiding places.

But members of the government were not the only ones who wanted an end to the situation in Crete where armed communists had been in hiding for almost a decade since the end of the civil war. In the elections in May 1958, EDA won 24% of the national vote and secured 79 of the 300 seats in Parliament. EDA was now the leading opposition party.

A rumour gradually spread through what was left of the communist movement in Crete that the Moscow-based central committee of the KKE had informed the EDA leadership that it intended to disband all its underground organisations in Greece and work legally through EDA.

In the autumn of 1959, Kostas Kasiotakis came from Athens with a note from the central committee of the KKE giving written confirmation of its decision to disband the underground organisation. Kasiotakis also brought a large sum of money, which the fugitives were to use to escape abroad. The order that the fugitives should leave Greece was unambiguous. Kokovlis gave Kasiotakis a note to take back to Athens, giving assurances that he intended to disband the organisation in Crete and leave the country with his fellow fugitives.

Kokovlis and Polychronaki set about printing leaflets for distribution to all their supporters, explaining that the clandestine organisation in Crete was disbanding and calling on all their comrades to support EDA in future. No mention was made of the fugitives' decision to try to leave the country.

On a moonless night at the end of 1959, the eight fugitives met up to discuss how they could escape abroad. The discussion had hardly started when two of them, George Tzobanakis and Spiro Blazakis, made it clear that they were going to stay in Crete whatever the others decided.

Despite the decision of Tzobanakis and Blazakis, the remaining six fugitives agreed to carry out the order they had been given and leave the country. They made plans to obtain identity cards and make their way to Athens individually or in pairs. The least known of the six were to depart first and on arrival in Athens were to begin planning for their onward journey to Italy.

Only the most trusted supporters were asked for their help in obtaining identity cards that had belonged to people who had recently died. Dates of birth on these cards were altered as necessary to pass a cursory inspection by the police.

In the summer of 1960, Kostas Lionakis left from Heraklion and was followed a few weeks later by Stamatis Mariolis, who took the boat for Piraeus from Souda. Shortly afterwards, Yanni Lionakis and Pagona Kokovli left from Heraklion and joined the others in a flat in an Athens suburb.

Kokovlis and Polychronaki took the overnight ferry from Souda to Piraeus in the spring of 1962 and on arrival were met by Yanni Lionakis and Pagona Kokovli. The four of them took a taxi to a basement flat, a KKE safe house, in which Mariolis and Kostas Lionakis were waiting to be reunited with them.

For the first time, the six fugitives enjoyed the strange experience of sitting around a table together in a comfortable, modern flat and chatting without having to keep their voices to a whisper. The four who had been in Athens for some time had already finalised plans for their journey to Italy. With the help of the Italian Communist Party they hoped to reach Eastern Europe. Their final destination was to be

Tashkent in Uzbekistan where, since the end of the civil war, 17,000 Greek communists had made their homes.

Late one afternoon in June 1962, the six took a bus to Glyphada and met a man that one of the fugitives had become acquainted with in a local bar. This man had made arrangements for the six to be taken to Italy by sea. The price demanded was a high one but no questions were asked and the two men who were to sail the boat were content to know only that the six needed to leave the country in secret.

It was early evening when the small boat left harbour and took the fugitives into exile.

Chapter 13
The Eagles of Crete

Following the communist defeat in the Samaria Gorge, George Tzobanakis and Spiro Blazakis had occasionally been in the same guerrilla band for short periods but had regularly split up and joined other groups. Over the years the guerrilla numbers dwindled and from the end of September 1954, at a time when there were just eleven fugitives still on the run in western Crete, the two men teamed up for good. In the early days they spent together they swore an oath that they would never be taken alive, and if one of them was wounded and about to be captured the other would kill him. They were to remain together for twenty years.

By day they usually hid in caves, coming out at night to meet a few comrades who fed them and supplied them with news, information and, occasionally, some new clothes. However, now and then they had no option but to take the olive oil that had been left by pious villagers for lighting the lamps in the country churches, or steal the odd lamb or goat from local farmers and shepherds. They were to insist in years to come that locals generally sympathised with them and understood the reason for the occasional theft, which was a matter of life or death to the fugitives.

All the hide-outs used by Blazakis and Tzobanakis had a difficult and dangerous access, made even more hazardous in heavy rain, which would stream down the rock face. In winter, during and after thunderstorms, the fugitives always took great care not to leave any tracks in the muddy ground for the gendarmes to find. They were also careful not to leave traces of mud on large boulders when they stepped over them. Keen-sighted shepherds and gendarmes, most of whom regularly hunted hare in their spare time, would have spotted this trail as easily as if it had been a trail of footprints in the snow. The fugitives also avoided damaging any thorny bushes that grew in abundance in the area around their caves, even though some of the routes they used were virtually choked with them.

Whenever they moved around at night there was always the risk that they would attract attention by accidentally kicking stones on the footpaths or knocking loose stones as they clambered over dry-stone walls. Apart from the gendarme patrols there were occasional goat thieves moving around at night who might spot the fugitives. When visiting a contact in a village they always waited an hour after the *kapheneion* closed to give the locals a chance to go to sleep. If all was quiet they knew there was no search party in the village: the dogs would always bark at strangers moving around. They then had to move very quietly themselves so as not to disturb the dogs and wake up the villagers.

One of the most hazardous activities the two men faced was approaching wells for water. Wells and country springs were the main sources of water available to men on the run, and the most likely places for search parties to set an ambush. To counter the danger of walking into an ambush, the fugitives would always wait a short distance away from a well and watch and listen in silence in the darkness for at least half an hour. Both men had acquired an acute sense of hearing from their years in hiding. The number of gendarmes in a search party would usually be between ten and twelve and, when given the task of spending a night in hiding around a well, few managed to do so without making a noise of some sort. Often a gendarme would call in a low voice to a nearby colleague, or another would light up a cigarette, or cough. Any one of these signs would give away the presence of the search party to the fugitives as they watched and waited in the darkness.

Sometimes the water they drank at the wells was not clean. This was a problem especially in summer when thirsty reptiles and rodents, in an attempt to drink from a well, would accidentally fall in and sink to the bottom. There they would rot and pollute the water. One night Tzobanakis was drinking some water he had just drawn from a well when he realised that something was floating in his tin mug. He moved to a secluded spot where he could shine a torch on the mug's contents and discovered half a rotting mouse floating on the surface of the water. On another occasion the pair returned to their cave with some water they intended to use to cook some rice. They were halfway through their meal before they found half a lizard in their cooking pot.

Rodents and reptiles were an unavoidable irritation in the caves. Food that was left lying around on plates was eaten by mice or, sometimes, by snakes. Mice would make holes in the knapsacks in an attempt to get at the bread they contained, or nibble the guerrillas' boots. The mice even ate the candles that were necessary to provide vital light. One cave the two men used frequently was so full of fleas that it was almost impossible for the fugitives to get any sleep. They managed to solve this particular problem by obtaining some DDT from one of their helpers and sprinkling it lavishly around the cave, ridding themselves of the fleas forever and enabling them to use the cave for years to come. But the fugitives could not rid themselves of the mice so easily and had to learn to live with them.

When drenched by rain, the fugitives were often forced to sit in damp caves in wet clothes all day long as they rarely had a change of clothing. Neither of the fugitives would have survived for long alone and both of them, not surprisingly, became seriously ill in the long years that they spent together on the run. They frequently relied on each other for support and were fortunate that whenever one of them was ill the other was always fit enough to look after his comrade. It was something of a miracle that the two fugitives were able to spend more than a quarter of a century living in such poor conditions without contracting serious, life-threatening illnesses.

One of their comrades, George Romanias, had died after eating poisoned food provided by a man he trusted. The two fugitives could never be quite certain that one of their helpers, tempted by the large reward on offer, would not do the same to them. The never-ending fear of betrayal preyed on their minds.

Having survived ill health and the constant threat of ambush or betrayal there was always the chance that one or other of the fugitives would succumb to a pure accident that would prove fatal. A broken leg or sprained ankle in a remote cave meant certain death, especially if the fugitives were moving around alone, as they occasionally did.

Exploring all the potholes in the caves they were using, however dangerous, was always essential: should gendarmes ever find and search a cave they were occupying, it would be vital for the fugitives to be able to retreat into a recess to escape detection. The two men had a poor opinion of gendarmes whose job it was to search caves for the fugitives, joking that they performed their task so fearfully that they were clearly terrified that they would come upon their cornered prey in the darkness.

Boredom, however, was their worst enemy. The lonely, monotonous years slipped by as the two men sat in their gloomy caves, in the bowels of the earth, often without the light of a candle.

Soon after winning the elections in 1964, Prime Minister George Papandreou amnestied almost all of the remaining communists who were still being held in custody. Encouraged by the new mood in the country, Tzobanakis and Blazakis anticipated an early end to their life on the run. However, no amnesty was granted to the two men.

Some Greeks were now allowed visas to meet relatives who had fled to the countries behind the Iron Curtain at the end of the civil war. News eventually reached Greece that six fugitives from Crete were living and working in Tashkent, confirming the government's suspicion that most of the remaining fugitives had successfully fled the country.

Nikos Kokovlis and Argiro Polychronaki had married and were working for the Greek newspaper, *Neos Dromos*, in Tashkent. Yanni Lionakis had married Pagona Kokovli, who was training to be a doctor. Costas Lionakis had married a local girl and Stamatis Mariolis had married Irini, a young woman from Palea Roumata. Irini's father had been killed during the civil war and her family had remained staunch supporters of the communist fugitives. In 1963, Irini left her village, telling everybody she was ill and going to seek medical treatment abroad. She went to Paris and from there flew via Moscow to Tashkent, where Mariolis was waiting for her.

As the two fugitives passed the time in their caves, great changes began to take place throughout Crete during the 1960s. Many young people chose to forsake the villages of their birth and settle in Athens where they hoped to find more opportunities of employment and a better life for themselves and their families. In this, they were often encouraged by their parents who saw Athens as a paradise where people lived a life of leisure compared to the tough life in the Cretan villages. Provided one family member stayed behind to help look after their property, parents accepted that the rest of their family must depart. Most of the young people who left the villages preferred the life in Athens and wrote to their friends back home, encouraging them to come to the capital. Workers were needed in Athens, especially on building sites, and high wages were being paid. As the young flocked to the capital, the villages became depopulated.

It was not until the late nineteen-sixties that the remoter villages of Crete received piped water and three dozen of the remotest villages in Canea prefecture - Kokkino Horio, Kefalas and Drakona amongst them - eventually received electricity. It was also at this time that many roads on the island were improved. The road to the Omalos Plateau was asphalted and a permit was issued for a small kiosk to open at the Omalos entrance to the Samaria Gorge. In December 1969 a mountain hut, with room to sleep 70, was opened on Kallergi hill, above the Samaria Gorge, where 22 years earlier the guerrillas had posted a lookout to give warning of approaching planes that occasionally came over on strafing and bombing raids.

In the early hours of 21 April 1967 a group of army officers seized power in Athens in a coup d'état. The army very quickly had a firm grip on the country and all leading figures considered likely to organise opposition to the regime were rounded up and imprisoned. An announcement was made forbidding the assembly of citizens, banning strikes and imposing a curfew from dusk to dawn.

When they had securely established themselves in power, the military government determined to eliminate the remaining communist fugitives in Crete. However, the increased number of search parties sent out to hunt for the two men met with no more success than previously. Eventually, in February 1968, the military government in

Athens published an offer of an amnesty for the two fugitives. The offer was valid for two months.

While the amnesty was on offer, senior army officers led large patrols through all the villages in Apokoronas. In every village they assembled the locals in the square and made speeches demanding an end to the help and support given to the fugitives who now had, they said, an opportunity to return to their homes and live amongst their law-abiding fellow men. Failure to accept the amnesty would prove to everybody that the fugitives were just common outlaws. The officers also issued a warning that if the fugitives failed to surrender then arrests and deportation of all their suspected supporters would follow immediately on the expiry of the amnesty offer.

As the deadline for the amnesty drew closer and the fugitives failed to give themselves up, a local priest and a teacher were prevailed upon to assist the military in making appeals to the people. A bus was provided to take them from village to village where they addressed the inhabitants. After calling upon the villagers to cease their support for the fugitives, they continued to the next village, where the inhabitants were already being assembled in the square by a platoon of soldiers who had gone ahead of them.

Tzobanakis and Blazakis ignored all calls for them to surrender and, after the time limit for the amnesty had expired, army officers returned with patrols to villages in Apokoronas and berated the inhabitants for not giving up the fugitives. Villagers suspected of harbouring or helping the fugitives were publicly insulted and threatened.

Eventually the government abandoned its plans to arrest villagers and the patrols became less hostile. The dictators in Athens did not give up their plan to eliminate the two communists but attempted a new approach, albeit one that had first been tried without success years earlier. A network of informers in the villages was built up, the amount of the reward was increased and assurances of well-paid employment and a good pension were made to anybody giving information that led to the capture, dead or alive, of the two men. Villagers grew suspicious of each other, not knowing whom they could trust or who might be in the pay of the police.

The Eagles of Crete

During the nineteen-sixties, Tzobanakis and Blazakis had become known as the Eagles of Crete and had acquired a wide circle of supporters, many of whom did not share their political ideology but felt a certain pity for the two men who had been in hiding for so long. Following the military coup in 1967, the two fugitives felt they could no longer count on all those who had helped them in the past. Instead, they were forced to rely on the few committed communists among their helpers. For much of the time the dictators were in power the fugitives rarely left their hide-outs until it was completely dark. All day and night was spent in darkness. Fearful of going blind, the two men would often crawl to cave entrances during the daytime and, when they considered it safe to do so, sit there and allow their eyes to experience the daylight for short periods.

In 1970 another attempt was made by the government in Athens to offer an amnesty to the two men. The dictators took the unusual step of sending a relative of one of the fugitives to Crete. As a rule, officials in a position of authority, such as senior police officers and judges, were debarred from serving in areas where they had grown up or had many relatives. This was solely in the interests of impartiality, for it was commonly believed that a senior official in a position of power would be obliged to show favouritism to relatives when carrying out his duties.

The announcement that Major-General Kiriakos Tzobanakis had arrived to serve in Canea aroused much curiosity among the locals, but the real reason for his appointment soon became apparent. He lost no time in summoning all adult male members of the Tzobanakis clan and well-known left-wingers from Apokoronas to his office for a personal chat. The major-general informed the assembled company that he had been appointed to Canea by the Athens government precisely because he was a distant relative of George Tzobanakis, who had now been wanted by the authorities for over twenty years. He wished to make contact with the fugitives in order to offer them an amnesty, which he would personally guarantee.

Despite the protests of all those he spoke to that they had no contact whatsoever with the fugitives and had no idea where they might be, the major-general gave each of them a copy of a letter for George Tzobanakis. In the letter he repeated the promises he had made to those who had been summoned to his office. He urged his cousin to send word that the two wished to accept the amnesty and promised that as soon as he heard that they were willing to take advantage of this offer, he would inform the government and see to it that the amnesty was granted and publicised in the press. The major-general would himself collect the fugitives, take them to his own home and ensure that they were provided with good employment and a safe, secure future.

By chance, one of those to whom the major-general gave a copy of the letter was in touch with the two fugitives. The two men, however, were distrustful of the dictators and suspected a trap so did nothing. Six months later the major-general repeated the process, using the same people to distribute a second letter. This met with no more success than the first, and a few months later Major-General Tzobanakis was recalled to Athens.

In 1973 there was growing opposition to the junta inside the country, with a mutiny in the navy in May and a sit-in organised by students at Athens Polytechnic in November. The mutiny was quickly suppressed and the junta leaders, convinced that the king was behind it, took steps to abolish the monarchy. The sit-in at the Polytechnic was violently broken up on 17 November when tanks stormed the campus. Police and soldiers cleared the buildings, killing and injuring many students. This action met with international condemnation and turned many previously loyal senior army officers against the junta.

The dictators finally resigned following the Turkish invasion of Cyprus in July 1974. Constantine Karamanlis returned from exile and formed a government. As prime minister, he immediately announced the release of all political prisoners and the restoration of citizenship and passports to those deprived of them by the junta. Legalisation of the KKE quickly followed.

The two fugitives in Crete were hopeful that they would be covered by the amnesty given to all political prisoners at this time, but the weeks dragged on and while their fellow countrymen celebrated the return of democracy, the fugitives remained in their caves.

One night a friend showed them a brief newspaper article, which stated that the fugitives in Crete were exempt from the amnesty recently granted to all political prisoners. The pair were shattered by the news and asked a reliable comrade to seek legal advice on their case from a left-wing lawyer. A few days later they received confirmation that the amnesty did not apply to them.

Many leading figures, including the composer Mikis Theodorakis, who had recently returned from exile in Paris, sought amnesty for the two fugitives. One point in their favour was that the two men had strongly opposed the dictatorship and had declined an amnesty offered by the junta.

But the new government was busy attempting to solve its many problems, the most pressing of which was the threat of war with Turkey over Cyprus. Other concerns were the new constitution, a referendum on the return of the monarchy and the arrest and trial of junta leaders and supporters. The year the junta fell was a disastrous one for the economy, with a dramatic drop in tourism, which earned much foreign currency for the country. Crete had welcomed 31,600 tourists in 1973 but in 1974 there were only 24,700 arrivals, and of these, 1,200 were West Germans who arrived in Maleme in October for a special service for the German war dead buried in the nearby cemetery. The government was clearly too busy to concern itself with the plight of the two fugitives.

Both men began to suffer from the increasing psychological pressure as each day passed with no announcement of a pardon. Journalists from Athens began to arrive on the island, all of them hoping to make contact with the fugitives and obtain an exclusive interview with them. The journalists drove from village to village chatting to the locals in every *kapheneion*, appealing to them to pass on their request to the fugitives for a meeting. The authorities kept a close eye on the journalists' movements, making any such meeting impracticable and the fugitives decided to keep their heads down and avoid all contact with them.

As the weeks dragged on, the two men changed their minds. In Athens there was a British journalist who had been trying to make contact with them for some time. From one of their acquaintances they learnt that the journalist, David Tonge, had written several articles that had been translated and published in *Pravda* and several Eastern European newspapers. Tonge also had the distinction of having been deported from Greece during the dictatorship. He had a reputation as a man of integrity and was thought to be genuinely sympathetic to their case. The fugitives decided to fix a meeting with him.

In late December 1974, arrangements were made for Tonge to visit Crete and meet the fugitives without attracting attention from the authorities. The fugitives chose a location for the rendezvous and the meeting was planned to take place late at night.

Tonge and his young female interpreter met their contact in a Canea backstreet just as it was beginning to grow dark. To make sure they were not being followed they were led through several deserted roads and lanes before getting into a waiting car. After a long drive into the mountains, the car stopped at a burnt-out house that had its windows covered. Tonge and his interpreter were taken inside and told to wait.

After a couple of hours the two fugitives, smartly dressed and clean-shaven, made a sudden, dramatic appearance. A man who had come with them remained outside the house to keep watch. Tzobanakis did most of the talking and occasionally he got so carried away with his reminiscences that the lookout came in to ask him to keep his voice down.

While it was still dark, the fugitives brought the meeting to an end. They explained that they had a long march to their hide-out in the mountains, and set off as soon as their lookout confirmed that the coast was clear. Tonge returned to Athens as inconspicuously as he had left and wrote his story for his paper.

Tonge's article attracted international sympathy for the plight of the two fugitives in Crete and their case was taken up once more with the Minister for Justice. Nonetheless, the Minister repeated his previous decision that the two fugitives were not covered by the 1974

The Eagles of Crete

amnesty for political prisoners and insisted that their crimes were not political but criminal. Members of Parliament of the Centre Party and New Democracy continued to raise the matter in Parliament, demanding a resolution to the affair. Sympathy for the fugitives increased as a rumour spread that one of the men was seriously ill and in need of urgent medical attention.

Two weeks later the government relented and announced that it would, after all, put a bill before parliament granting an amnesty to the two Cretan fugitives. This amnesty, the Minister of Justice stressed, was to apply only to the two men in Crete and not to any of those who had fled abroad. Ten days later the amnesty was published in the government gazette. It was granted on condition that if either of the men committed a crime within the next three years that carried a prison sentence of more than one year, the amnesty for their previous crimes would be null and void. The date set for Blazakis and Tzobanakis to receive their amnesty was Saturday 22 February 1975.

Officials of the KKE in Canea sent a message to the two fugitives to let them know that they would collect them at a time and place of their choosing and arrange a small ceremony with some of their supporters and journalists to celebrate their freedom. The two men informed the KKE leaders that they would be somewhere in the Therisso Gorge at mid-morning on Sunday 23 February and that they would show themselves when they saw their welcoming party approach. The meeting place was kept a secret, and even the KKE officials did not know the exact point in the gorge where the men would be waiting. Local radio speculated that the two men would make their appearance in Kokkino Horio.

The night before they were to meet their supporters and the press, Tzobanakis and Blazakis could hardly sleep as they anticipated the change in their lives that the following day would bring. From being hunted men living in damp caves they were about to face the international media and be free, at last, to roam wherever they chose. They discussed, as they had on many previous occasions, their plan to visit Moscow and see the land of their dreams.

Early the next morning the two men were in position, sitting on the hillside hidden behind some bushes, waiting patiently for their welcoming committee. It was around 10.30 when they heard and then saw a convoy of cars and trucks coming up the gorge. Just as the lead car passed their position they fired two shots in the air and the convoy came to a halt. The two men skipped down the mountain to join their supporters, finally putting an end to their time in hiding, which had lasted almost three decades.

There was much hugging and backslapping as the two men were met with affection they had not known for many years. The widow of *Kapetan* Mihali presented the two men with bunches of red carnations. Blazakis read out a short statement paying tribute to their comrades who had fallen in the civil war and thanking the politicians of all parties who had raised their case in Parliament. At the end of Blazakis' brief speech the assembled crowd sang resistance songs dating back to the German occupation. The convoy then drove to the Hotel Kydon in Canea.

Awaiting them at the hotel was another throng of well-wishers and the appearance of the two men was met with loud cheering. Blazakis and Tzobanakis made their way into the hotel lounge where a group of Greek and foreign journalists was assembled. The two men were delighted to give a press conference and answer the reporters' questions.

One of the first things that the men made clear was that they had rejected all offers of amnesty over the years as they considered it dishonourable to sign a declaration of repentance renouncing their ideological convictions. The pair described how they had spent their years in hiding, often going without food for two days at a time. During their early years on the run, life had been very tough and they had quickly adapted to doing everything by night. So accustomed were they to walking in the dark that they never once lost their way or stumbled on the wild, trackless mountains. From 1960 they had had a radio and to alleviate the boredom they had read whatever books or papers came to hand.

Tzobanakis lovingly displayed some of the contents of his knapsack for the assembled audience. The first item he produced was a pair

The Eagles of Crete

of hair clippers, which he held aloft. There followed some tins of fish and a bundle of sage that they had picked high in the White Mountains. The sage, Tzobanakis explained, would be taken by both men to Athens and placed at the gates of the Polytechnic in memory of the students who had lost their lives while opposing the dictatorship.

At the end of the press conference, the two men, accompanied by a few close friends in half a dozen cars, set off for their villages. They stopped briefly in Gavalohori and then continued to Kokkino Horio, where such a huge crowd had gathered in anticipation of seeing them that the gendarmes from the nearby post at Vamos had arrived in force to keep order. The two men ignored the gendarmes, who until recently had been charged with their capture, and walked to the village square, greeted on all sides by young and old.

Tzobanakis' sister was expecting them at her house, where she had tables laden with food and carafes of wine. All those who could do so crammed into her home, some seated at the tables and the rest standing. An evening of eating, drinking and singing followed and it was very late when Tzobanakis and Blazakis were driven back to the Hotel Kydon where a room had been reserved for the two men that night.

Completely exhausted, the two men finally retired to their room, hoping to get a good night's sleep. They had not slept well recently in anticipation of the day that would mark an end to their time on the run and a return to living a normal life. That day had finally arrived and the two men who had spent decades hiding in the remotest parts of Crete took their first hot showers and prepared themselves for bed in one of the most modern and comfortable hotels in Canea.

But despite their tiredness they were unable to get to sleep. They had exchanged their peaceful mountains for the centre of Canea, and for almost the whole night were kept awake by the noise of the town's traffic.

BIBLIOGRAPHY

In English

Averoff-Tossizza, Evangelos, *By Fire and Axe*, Caratzas Brothers, New York, 1978
Beevor, Antony, *Crete:The Battle and Resistance*, John Murray, 1991
Brindakis, George, *Canea 27/5/1941 – 23/5/1945*, Michalis Yeorvasakis O.E, 1996
Buckley, Christopher, *Greece and Crete 1941*, Efstathiadis, 1977
Clark, Alan, *The Fall of Crete*, Anthony Blond, 1962
Elliot, Murray, *Vasili - the Lion of Crete*, Stanley Paul, 1987
Fielding, Xan, *The Stronghold*, Secker, 1953
Fielding, Xan, *Hide and Seek*, Secker, 1954
Harakopos, George, *Fortress Crete, 1941-44*, B. Giannikos and Co, 1993
Kokonas, N.A, *The Cretan Resistance 1941–1945*, Rethymnon, 1992
Kokovlis, Nikos and Argiro, *Underground*, Translated by Thomas Tunberg, Unpublished, 1997
Panayiotakis, George, *Documents From the Battle and Resistance of Crete 1941–1945*, G. Detorakis, Heraklion, 2000
Rendel, Alexander M, *Appointment in Crete*, Allan Wingate, London, 1953
Richter, Heinz, *British Intervention in Greece* (trans. Marion Sarafis), Merlin, 1985

In Greek

Bandouraki–Boleti, Eleftheria, *Taxidevoun Stin Ionia Ta Onira Mas*, Germanos, Thessaloniki, 1999
Blazakis, Spiro and Tzobanakis, George, *35 Khronia Antistasi*, Gramak EPE Athens, 1976

Iliakis, Lefteris, *O Emfilios Polemos stin Kriti*, Canea, 2002
Iliakis, Lefteris, *I Antistasi sto N. Khanion*, Canea 2003
Karvounakis, Michali G, *Me to ELAS sta Lefka Ori*, Athens, 2000
Kokovlis, Nikos and Argiro, *ESSD Prosdokies kai Pragmatikotita*, Mnimes,1986
Kokovlis, Nikos and Argiro, *Mnimes Pou Pote Then Svinoun*, Canea, 1994
Kokovlis, Nikos and Argiro, *Allos Dromos Then Ipirkhe*, Polytupo, Athens, 2002
Manousakas, Yannis, *O Fugodikos*, Odysseas, 1980
Manousakas, Yannis, *Emfilios Sti Skia tis Akronafplias*, Dodoni, 1986
Margarites, George, *Istoria tou Ellenikou Emfiliou Polemou*, Vivliorama, 2001
Madarites, N & A, *Sta Vouna Tis Kritis kai Stin Paranomia*, 70-Planitis. 1979
Perakakis, Nikos M, *Iroes kai Martires*, Milopotamos, 1978
Perakakis, Nikos M, *I Kriti stis Floges*, Athens, 1979
Perakakis, Nikos M, *I Nei Khainides*, Athens, 1979
Proimos, Stephanos, *O ELAS tis Kritis*, Athens, 1989
Tsivis, Yannis, *Katokhi kai Antistasi*, Gnosi, 1985
Vlandas, M, *I Prodomeni Epanastasi 1941 – 44*, Evangelios, Athens, 1977
Vlisidis, D and Iliakis, L, *Ta Prota Vimata tou EAM stin Kriti*, Canea, 1997
Vlontakis, Stavros, *I Okhira Thesis Kritis*, Athens, 1975

LOCAL NEWSPAPERS

Dimokratia	1946 – 47
Nea Epohi	1946 – 65
Paratiritis	1942 – 44 and 1947 – 66
Kyrix	1947 - 1975
Haniotika Nea	1967 - 1975

List of Main Characters

Bandourakis, Yanni	ELAS *kapetan* during the occupation; commander of a large band of guerrillas in the civil war
Baras, Argiris	From Vasilika, Khalkidhiki; one of the soldiers who defected from the army camp at Agios Nikolaos to join Podias
Bandouvas, Manoli	Wealthy landowner from Ano Asites with his own private army; republican, anti-communist
Blazakis, Spiro	From Gavalohori; served in Albania, where he developed frostbite; member of ELAS and the Democratic Army
Boloudakis, Christos	*Kapetan* in ELAS and the Democratic Army
Douroundakis, Adonis	From Hordaki, Akrotiri; a member of ELAS, he did not take part in the civil war; joined Agia Triada monastery on Akrotiri as a monk and later became the archimandrite
Fielding, Major Alexander	British officer, served in western Crete from January 1942 – August 1942 and from November 1942 – January 1944
Gyparis, Lt Colonel Pavlos	Republican army officer who led a special force against the communists in 1947-48
Hatzigrigoris, Stavros	A lawyer; took to the mountains in 1947
Kladou, Vangelio	From Anogia; a member of EPON and later of the central committee of the KKE in Crete; took to the mountains in 1948

Kodelas, George	From Corinth, a major with ELAS in the Peloponnese during the occupation; leader of a band of guerrillas in Kissamos and Selino during the civil war; known as Kapetan George
Kodonidis, Xenophon	Member of ELAS; led a small band of guerrillas in the civil war; died in the mountains
Kokovlis, Nikos	Born in Asia Minor; a member of EAM in Canea during the occupation; took to the mountains in 1947
Kondekakis, Colonel Gregory	Replaced General Mandakas as commander of ELAS forces in Crete in December 1943
Koutalonis, Vassili	A guerrilla from Drakona
Mandakas, General Manoli	ELAS leader in Crete; did not take part in the civil war
Manousakas, Yanni	Escaped from Corfu prison in 1943; appointed military leader in Crete at the beginning of the civil war
Manousakis, Nikos	Escapee from Folegandros; senior EAM leader on Crete from 1941-44; died of TB in March 1945
Manousellis, George	An ELAS *kapetan* from Kallikratis; leader of a small group of guerrillas in the civil war
Mariolis, Stamatis	From Sparta in the Peloponnese; an aircraftsman at Maleme, joined the Democratic Army
Mitsotakis, Constantine	A member of EOK; newspaper owner; elected Liberal MP in Crete in 1946; Prime Minister of Greece 1990-93
Papapanayiotakis, Mihali	Served in ELAS in Roumeli during the occupation and rose to the rank of colonel; took to the mountains at the

	beginning of the civil war and replaced Manousakas as commander of the guerrilla force on Crete; known as *Kapetan Mihali*
Papayannakis, Major Dimitri	Commander of the Special Gendarme Battalion raised by the Germans in 1944
Pissadakis, Manoli	Escapee from Folegandros; leader of one of the first ELAS bands in the White Mountains; arrested in February 1944 and spent the rest of the war in a concentration camp in Germany; a leading *kapetan* in the civil war
Podias, Yanni	A refugee from Asia Minor; ELAS *kapetan* on Mt Ida during the occupation; leader of the guerrillas in Eastern Crete in the civil war
Polychronaki, Argiro	From Drakona, joined her brother in the White Mountains in 1947 and remained there after he surrendered
Sbokos, George	A lawyer by profession; led a small communist band on Mt Ida
Schubert, Fritz	Employed by the Germans as leader of a special unit of collaborators
Siganos, Dr Manoli	Serving time in Acronauplia prison when the Germans invaded, sent to prison in northern Greece, he escaped and worked with EAM until the end of the war; appointed a member of the central committee of the KKE in Crete in 1947
Skevaki, Georgia	From Trialonia, Kissamos; leader of the female guerrillas in the White Mountains
Skoulas, Nikos	Mayor of Canea; EOK representative
Tsamantis, Nikos	*Kapetan* of an ELAS band during the occupation; guerrilla leader in the White Mountains in the civil war

Tsitilos, George	Worked for EAM in the Peloponnese during the German occupation; replaced Vlandas as EAM leader in Crete in 1946
Tzobanakis, George	From Kokkino Horio; fought in the Battle of Crete at Heraklion; a member of ELAS and the Democratic Army
Vlandas, Mitsos	Escapee from Gavdos; EAM leader on Crete from 1944-46
Bishop Xirouhakis	Born in Souri in Apokoronas, studied in Italy and spent fifteen years at Agia Triada church in Vienna, spoke fluent Italian and German; Bishop of Kidonia and Apokoronas

Glossary

Acronauplia Prison	A large prison in the old Venetian castle in Nauplion, which at the outbreak of war with Germany was home to 600 communist prisoners; also known as 'Karl Marx University' as many prisoners received a communist education from other inmates while serving time there
EAM	Ethnikon Apeleftherotikon Metopon = National Liberation Front
EDA	Eniaia Dimokratiki Aristera = United Democratic Left
ELAS	Ethnikos Laikos Apeleftherotikos Stratos = National Popular Liberation Army
EOK	Ethniki Organosis Kriton = National Organisation of Cretans
EPON	Ethniki Panelladiki Organosis Neolaias = National Panhellenic Youth Organisation
Kapheneion	cafe
Kapetan	A military title given to a leader who commanded a local armed following
KKE	Kommounistikon Komma Ellados = Communist Party of Greece
Kokovlis, Nikos/Kokovli, Pagona	It is the custom in Crete to drop the final 's' for the female surname

MAY	Monades Asphaleias Ypaithrou = Units for the Defence of the Countryside
Omalos Plateau	A large plateau in the White Mountains; guerrilla base for much of the civil war
Prefectures/Provinces	Crete is divided into four prefectures (nomoi): Canea, Rethymnon, Heraklion and Lasithi. Each prefecture is subdivided into provinces (eparhies). For example, Canea prefecture has five provinces (Kissamos, Kidonia, Apokoronas, Sfakia and Selino).
Security Battalions	Greeks who fought for the Germans against ELAS
UNNRA	United Nations Relief and Rehabilitation Administration

Printed in Great Britain
by Amazon